Simplified Living

A 3-Step Proven Process To Simplify Your Home

TIFFANY WHEELER

Copyright © 2025 Tiffany Wheeler

All rights reserved. No part of this publication may be reproduced, distributed, or transmitted in any form or by any means—electronic, mechanical, photocopying, recording, or otherwise—without prior written permission from the publisher, except in the case of brief quotations embodied in critical reviews and certain other noncommercial uses permitted by copyright law.

For permission requests, contact: Tiffany Wheeler, tiffany@hivehouse.co

ISBN: 979-8-218-86010-3

Editor: Alexis Frueh

Photography credits: Tiffany Wheeler, Megan Wheeler, Wild Rose Photography, Cate Black, Sarah Hovenkamp, SOLiD Real Estate Photography, & Andrew Roberts

Cover Design: Sydney Rouse

<u>Disclaimer</u>
This book is for informational and inspirational purposes only. The author and publisher are not responsible for any actions taken based on the content of this work. Readers should use their own judgment and seek professional advice when necessary.

<u>Trademark Notice:</u>
Simplified Living™ is a registered trademark. To simplify the reading experience, the ™ symbol does not appear throughout the text. Its absence should not be interpreted as a waiver of any trademark rights.

Dedication

For anyone who has carried the weight of a cycle they did not create,

could not control,

or were never shown how to navigate—

you are loved.

May this book encourage you to let go of what weighs you down

and remind you that you are enough.

Acknowledgments

This book has been years in the making, and I would not have reached this point without the people who poured into me, supported me, and believed in the vision of *Simplified Living*.

To my family—Kim and our extended tribe—thank you for your patience, encouragement, and love through every late night and early morning. You are my why, and your steady belief in me has kept this dream alive.

To my Hivehouse Co. team—Lexi, Alexis, Sydney, Rachel, and Megan. You've not only helped me shape a business but have held space for a philosophy to become a lifestyle. Your creativity, dedication, and countless hours have brought *Simplified Living* to life in ways that reflect the very heart of what we stand for: women supporting women.

To Lexi, my OG believer, daughter-in-law, mother to two of our six grandchildren, and entrepreneurial mentor—thank you for giving me the courage to follow my dreams of becoming a business owner. You inspire me daily with your energy, creativity, and healthy outlook on life.

To Alexis, my editor, business mentor, and friend—your thoughtful guidance, steady encouragement, and gift for seeing the bigger picture have shaped not only this book, but also my growth as a leader and creative. Thank you for walking beside me through every draft, idea, and chapter of this journey.

To Sydney, my brander, graphic designer, and the visionary behind our now-iconic stacked-chairs logo—you saw the potential in Hivehouse Co. from the very beginning and listened closely to my vision for where this company could go. Thank you for believing, refining, and curating the most beautiful branding a girl with a dream could ask for.

To Rachel—my sister-in-law, fashionista, makeup goddess, table-for-two foodie, stylist, and lover of all things unique—you are the yin to my yang in this creative grind. Thank you for always bringing your magic touch and blooming right when it matters most.

To Megan—my beautiful and talented niece who has poured countless hours into capturing what Hivehouse Co. does best—

your eye for beauty, your dedication on install days, and your thoughtful organization of every image that fills these pages mean more than words can say. You are deeply loved, and I can't thank you enough.

To the clients and friends who trusted me to walk alongside them in transforming their homes—your stories and courage are woven into these pages. This book is as much yours as it is mine.

To my incredible beta readers—thank you for lending your time, insight, and honest feedback to help refine these pages. Your thoughtful suggestions deepened the clarity, connection, and balance woven throughout this book. I'm grateful for the way you saw the heart of *Simplified Living* and helped me bring it forward with intention.

And finally, to you, the reader—thank you for opening these pages and letting Simplified Living guide you. I hope that it gives you the courage to create a home and a life that reflects who you are and the way you want to live.

With gratitude,

Tiffany Wheeler

Founder of Hivehouse, Co.

"

Simplified Living isn't about less— it's about more of what matters.

Simplified Living
Creating Space for What Truly Matters

Behind the Buzz: The Journey to Hivehouse Co.

At Hivehouse Co., we are deeply inspired by the intricate yet organized world of bees. Just as bees curate their hives with purpose and precision, we believe every home should reflect this same level of simplicity, efficiency, and intention. Our philosophy, deeply rooted in the natural rhythms of life, embraces the idea that a well-maintained space fosters creativity, tranquility, and a stronger connection to our daily lives, mirroring bees' meticulous care for their hives.

My fascination with bees began long before Hivehouse Co. existed. Their rhythm—equal parts work and rest—reminded me that harmony doesn't mean perfection. It means everything has a purpose and a place, even in the busiest season of life. That same balance became the foundation of my work and my life.

Minimalism isn't just about having fewer things—it's about creating an environment that nurtures clarity, purpose, and well-being. It's about shifting our mindset from one of accumulation to one of intentionality, where everything in our space has meaning and supports the life we truly want to live. Through Hivehouse Co., I've learned that the journey to simplifying is often just as emotional as it is physical, and that embracing simplicity is a deeply personal process.

Minimalism focuses on less; *Simplified Living* focuses on enough. Enough isn't a number—it's a feeling: steady, breathable, aligned. When we name what is enough, we stop negotiating with clutter and start calibrating for balance. That shift—from removal to alignment—became the foundation of my work.

Simplifying is not just about tidying up physical items; it's about redefining our relationship with our surroundings. By stripping away the excess, we create spaces that cultivate inspiration, harmony, and genuine connections with those we love. In a world overwhelmed by consumerism and chaos, Hivehouse Co. champions a return to the essentials, focusing only on what truly enhances our lives—just as bees prioritize the most vital components of their hive.

The more I simplified, the more I noticed how deeply my environment affected my inner world. Each cleared surface, each intentional choice felt like an exhale—proof that less clutter outside meant more peace within. A moment of honesty: My turning point wasn't pretty. It was a Tuesday night, I was on the pantry floor looking at an expensive gadget I never used and feeling that familiar squeeze of guilt. I kept hearing, "But I should keep it." When I finally let it go, the relief surprised me. That single shelf felt lighter—and so did I. That was the first time I realized *Simplified Living* isn't about less; it's about removing what's heavy so balance can return.

This book is the first of many dedicated to minimal and intentional living principles. Drawing from my experience of simplifying and designing numerous homes, I have learned that simplifying a space can be a transformative and liberating experience. Whether you're beginning your simplifying journey for the first time or refreshing your current space, I hope this book provides the clarity, purpose, and sense of community needed to make lasting changes.

Before we dive into the methods and strategies that form the backbone of Hivehouse Co., let's take a step back to where it all began—with an unexpected turn of events that reshaped my entire perspective on home and community.

The path to balance began long before the first client consultation—it started in a storm that reminded me what it means to rebuild with intention.

TABLE OF CONTENTS

The Birth of Hivehouse Co.	11
The Hivehouse Co. Philosophy & The Simplified Living Method	21
The Mindset of Simplifying	33
The Six-Week Simplify Challenge	45
Week 1: The Foundation of Simplifying	55
Week 2: Living Rooms	67
Week 3: Personal Spaces	83
Week 4: Workspaces	109
Week 5: Kitchens & Storage	129
Week 6: Community & Giving Back	149
Designing with Purpose	165
Inspired by Nature	179
Simplified Living: Beyond the Home	193
Conclusion	203
Author's Note	207

The Birth of Hivehouse Co.

The Birth of Hivehouse Co.

From Chaos to Community

Hi! I'm Tiffany Wheeler, proud founder of Hivehouse Co.—though it didn't start out that way. Back in the early days, we called it *The Hive Method*. But before the name, the team, or the movement, there was a moment that planted the seed for this journey: Austin's infamous Winter Storm Uri in 2021.

It's funny how the most chaotic moments in life often reveal what we're meant to build. The living room became a shared drop-off zone and gathering spot. Wet socks steaming by the fire, Lego piles migrating across the rug, mugs sweating on the windowsill. The house breathed in and out—crying, teething babies, kettle whistling, laughter bursting out loud. In that noise, a strange calm: every person mattered, every task had a place. It felt, for the first time, like a hive—not perfect, but purposeful.

It all started when our son, Matthew, had a burst pipe that turned his home into an impromptu water park. Without hesitation, we opened our home to Matthew, his wife Lexi, and our teething grandsons, George and Louie. Just as we thought we had reached our hosting capacity, the storm knocked out our neighbor's power, and suddenly we were hosting a full-on "snowpocalypse sleepover." Every room, every corner, and what felt like every nook and cranny of our home was taken. And let me tell you, the gas fireplace became the hottest spot in town for five frosty days, keeping our makeshift village toasty and tight-knit.

Looking back, that storm became my first real lesson in balance—how chaos, when met with grace, can turn into an unexpected community.

As someone who finds comfort in solitude, the sudden influx of people was overwhelming at first. Coming from a family so small that we could all fit in a selfie, I was used to quiet spaces and personal retreats.

My idea of a perfect evening? A cozy blanket, a gripping murder mystery, and a perfectly mixed gin and tonic. My wife, Kim, however, was the complete opposite.

The ninth child in a lively, bustling household, she was born into a world where a full house was the norm. She thrived in the energy of a crowd and quickly helped me see the beauty in it. She showed me the magic of connection, laughter, and shared spaces—a perspective that would soon shape the foundation of *Hivehouse Co.*

A Quiet *Beginning*

Before Hivehouse Co.—before that snowy afternoon when ideas poured out faster than the coffee could cool—design was already quietly finding me. When I was ten, my dad built me a desk that stretched nearly the length of my bedroom wall, ten feet of promise framed in wood. Above it, he covered the wall in corkboard—a blank expanse waiting to be filled.

I filled it slowly, piece by piece: Meg Ryan's effortless smile, Julia Roberts's wild hair, Diane Keaton in her crisp trousers. Between them, I pinned pages from my mom's Better Homes & Gardens and the clean, sunlit lines of homes from Architectural Digest. There were clippings from Seventeen and Vogue, too, and a few movie stills where Pierce Brosnan or Patrick Dempsey grinned from the edges. Even then, I was drawn to the mix of story, style, and soul—how beauty could hint at something more profound.

That wall became my first vision board, though I didn't know to call it that. I was curating a world that felt steady and full of possibility. In a time when my family was shifting and life felt unpredictable, that room—lined with color, texture, and hope—became my first real project. It was how I made sense of things: arranging, layering, bringing order to what felt uncertain.

Looking back, it was never just a childhood bedroom. It was the first glimpse of what would one day become Hivehouse Co.—a quiet study in balance and belonging. What began as a way to create calm in the middle of change became a lifelong pursuit: beauty that steadies you, simplicity that holds you, and spaces that help you breathe again.

The Spark of *an Idea*

While Kim and Matthew took the boys on a snowy adventure, Lexi and I stayed back, sipped our elevated coffees, and finally had a rare moment of uninterrupted conversation. If you can picture two giddy women brain-dumping six months' worth of thoughts, you can imagine the energy in the room. Our chat started with the basics of simplifying, but quickly evolved, touching on everything from the structure of well-organized homes, bees and their habits, our shared love for the color yellow, and my passion for styling and design. We were all over the place yet completely in sync. That afternoon felt electric—like the creative kind of chaos that always comes before something meaningful.

That conversation quickly snowballed into bigger ideas—how homes could feel lighter, how letting go could be freeing, and how design choices could make daily life easier. We tossed around words like simplify, refresh, and revive, scribbling notes that soon became the beginnings of a method.

On the page, it looked like this, circled and underlined: Declutter → Organize → Style. In the margins: revive, refresh, renew; enough; balance; women supporting women. It wasn't just a checklist—it became a framework for balance, a tangible path toward spaces that breathe again.

We also dug into clutter itself: the mental weight it carries and how overwhelming it can feel. Lexi shared how chaos at home left her drained, and I understood immediately. I'd been there too—stuck in guilt, paralyzed by sentiment, unsure of where to start—before building small habits that kept my own space calm.

Together, we reflected on that emotional toll and began sketching out a step-by-step approach, not just to clear out stuff, but to truly transform our homes and our lives. We realized that simplifying wasn't just about letting go—it was about finding balance between what you own and what owns you.

> "
> Community changes how you experience chaos.

Not long after, Lexi's sister Maggie joined us, and the three of us dove into our first real project: transforming Lexi's cluttered home into a cozy short-term rental.

That project lit the spark—it grew into a six-week simplifying challenge, which then expanded into a Facebook group where people shared their mess, their progress, and their victories. What started as one family project quickly became a ripple effect—a reminder that when women support each other, transformation multiplies.

In those early days, we tossed around words like simplify, refresh, and revive, trying to capture the spirit of what we were building. That spontaneous, late-night brainstorming session became the foundation of what we called *The Hive Method*.

What began as one home reset evolved into a movement: a growing community where stories of messy playrooms, overflowing closets, and "if-you-know-you-know" shoe collections turned into camaraderie, encouragement, and ultimately, a shared desire to give back. It wasn't just about beautiful rooms—it was about meaningful rhythms.

With the support of Teifke Real Estate, our biggest cheerleaders and true EnTREpreneurs™, we co-hosted a garage sale in Round Rock, Texas. It was more than just a sale—it was a community coming together to revive, refresh, and renew their spaces. And just like that—bee-hold!—*The Hive Method* was officially born.

What began as a casual, coffee-fueled chat—and even a snowstorm survival story—grew into something far bigger. Minimalism wasn't just about creating an organized home; it was about changing how we lived. Simplified Living became more than a strategy—it was a lifestyle, a way to reclaim our homes, routines, and peace of mind. I realized this wasn't just about organizing stuff. *Simplified Living means creating space for what truly matters.*

As the work grew, so did the vision. *The Hive Method* gave us our start, but over time, we realized it wasn't just a method—it was a mindset. What resonated most wasn't the steps themselves, but the freedom people felt when they gave themselves permission to keep what mattered, let go of guilt, and design spaces that supported real life. That shift in perspective became the foundation for our next evolution—and the heart of Hivehouse Co.

And just like that, Hivehouse Co. was born. What I didn't realize then was that the same balance the bees had shown me—the one I built Hivehouse Co. on—would come to guide every design, every space, and eventually, every season of life.

Fun Fact

> My favorite singer-songwriter, Brandi Carlile, along with her fellow Highwomen, Natalie Hemby and Maren Morris, perfectly capture who we are as a modern family in their song "Crowded Table"—generous, hardworking, and the heart of every block party. This beautifully written song narrates the tale of forging a community amidst challenges. If you haven't graced your ears with Carlile's voice, you're bypassing a musical legend—pure magic.

The Hivehouse Co. Philosophy & The Simplified Living Method

The Hivehouse Co. Philosophy & The Simplified Living Method

The Evolution of Hivehouse Co.

Fast forward to the summer of 2023—what an exhilarating, creative journey it has been! What started as a casual conversation over coffee, a few scribbled ideas, and a living room brainstorming session has now blossomed into something far greater than I ever imagined. Hivehouse Co. was no longer just a business or a concept—it was a movement, a thriving community, and a way of life for those seeking clarity, order, and a renewed sense of purpose in their homes. What began as organizing rooms became a deeper calling: helping others find balance where chaos once lived. I realized that simplifying a home isn't just design—it's healing.

Looking back, the path from that first simplifying challenge to the fully realized Hivehouse Co. brand has been filled with passion, trial and error, and some truly unforgettable moments. From hosting community garage sales to building an engaged online family of like-minded individuals, every step has reinforced what I knew deep down—this wasn't just about getting rid of stuff. It was about creating space for what truly matters.

And while Hivehouse Co. continues to evolve, this moment is about you—the reader—ready to simplify, reset, and rediscover balance in your own life. Right now, let's focus on you and the reason you picked up this book in the first place.

You're here because you want to simplify—to clear the clutter and to embrace a life that feels lighter, freer, and more intentional. Along the way, something kept surfacing in our work: the idea of enough.

Enough space to breathe.
Enough structure to create calm.
Enough beauty to feel inspired.

Not less for the sake of less. Not perfect for the sake of appearances. But enough. That realization became the heartbeat of what we now call *Simplified Living*.

Simplified Living
Creating Space for What Truly Matters

Simplified Living isn't about stark minimalism or empty rooms—it's about living with *enough*. It's about curating spaces that support your lifestyle, reflect your values, and bring clarity and calm into your everyday life. Too often, simplifying is seen as "just getting rid of stuff," but at Hivehouse Co., we know it's much more. It's about creating space for what truly matters—whether that's meaningful connection, personal growth, or simply having a home that feels like a functional sanctuary.

The Hivehouse Co. philosophy was built upon *The Simplified Living Method*, which revolves around three essential steps: Simplify, Organize, and Style. These steps align with our original principles—Revive, Refresh, and Renew—into a clear, actionable framework designed to transform your home and support your life.

Step 1. Simplify
Edit with Intention

Over time, our homes collect more than just things—they collect emotional weight. Every item we own takes up space—not just physically, but mentally and emotionally. Simplifying is about editing with intention: releasing what no longer serves you, keeping what supports your life today, and allowing yourself to experience the freedom of a lighter, more functional space. This is the equivalent of reviving your home—returning it to a place of balance and energy.

Ways to Bee-gin

- ❖ Take inventory of what you own and ask yourself, *Does this add value to my life?*

- ❖ Start small: one drawer, one shelf, one space at a time.

- ❖ Use the "joy test": if an item no longer brings you joy or serves a purpose, let it go.

- ❖ Release guilt: by remembering, letting go makes room for what matters.

- ❖ Donate, sell, or repurpose to give unused items new life elsewhere.

Step 2. Organize
Create Flow

Once the excess is gone, organizing creates the systems that keep life flowing. Organization isn't about pretty bins—it's about designing solutions that fit your routines and make daily tasks easier. It's about finding efficient storage solutions, designating places for essential items, and ensuring that everything in your home has a purpose and a proper place. This is where calm becomes sustainable, and your home works with you, rather than against you.

Ways to Bee-gin

- ❖ Give frequently used items a consistent, logical home.
- ❖ Use bins, baskets, and dividers to create defined storage solutions.
- ❖ Build simple, maintainable systems: such as a mail station, a labeled pantry, or a functional entryway setup.
- ❖ Group like items together to reduce searching and stress.

Step 3. Style
Design with Purpose

Styling brings everything full circle—the fun part where your home reflects your personality, values, and aesthetic preferences. It's not about adding more or filling shelves with decor for the sake of it, but about curating with purpose.

Through color, light, texture, and meaningful details, you create an environment that feels intentional, comfortable, and uniquely yours. Thoughtful style renews your connection to your home, ensuring that the space you've worked so hard to simplify and organize continues to inspire and support your daily life.

Ways to Bee-gin

- ❖ Choose a palette that feels calm, inviting, or energizing—whatever supports your lifestyle.
- ❖ Rearrange furniture to improve flow and functionality.
- ❖ Create intentional zones: a cozy reading nook, a reset-ready entryway, or a place to recharge.
- ❖ Surround yourself with items that hold meaning rather than just taking up space.

A Note on Enough

Simplified Living began as a method, but it has grown into so much more—a philosophy, a lifestyle, and the heartbeat of Hivehouse Co. It's about creating balance: spaces that function, routines that flow, and style that reflects your story.

As you move forward, remember: this isn't about stripping life down to nothing. It's about building a foundation of enough—enough clarity, enough calm, and enough beauty to support the life you're living today.

People weren't looking for less. They were looking for enough.

The Mindset of Simplifying

The Mindset of Simplifying

Simplifying begins in the mind long before it happens in the home. The hardest part isn't deciding what to do with the drawer of takeout menus or the stack of old T-shirts—it's confronting the emotions tied to those things. Behind every item is a story: a gift from someone we love, a reminder of who we used to be, or a purchase we regret but feel obligated to keep.

This chapter is about untangling those stories. It's about giving yourself permission to keep what truly matters, releasing the guilt tied to the rest, and creating a new way of seeing your belongings. When you shift your mindset, the process of simplifying also shifts. Instead of loss, you'll see freedom. Instead of emptiness, you'll see space for what matters most.

The Emotional Side of Clutter

Simplifying isn't just about cleaning—it's about confronting the emotions tied to our possessions. Clutter isn't just piles of paper or overstuffed closets—it's a weight that sits on our shoulders and our hearts. Many of us don't realize how much our belongings are tied to our emotions until we try to let something go.

Guilt: *"It was a gift. I should keep it."*

Nostalgia: *"This reminds me of that trip, that relationship, that moment."*

Fear: *"What if I need it someday?"*

These feelings are entirely normal. But when they dictate what stays in our homes, they leave us surrounded by things that no longer serve us. Over time, that physical clutter becomes emotional clutter—an invisible drag on our energy, our mood, and even our relationships.

Here's the good news: clutter isn't a character flaw. It's a conversation between who you were, who you thought you should be, and who you are right now. Simplifying invites you to close the loop on old stories and choose the one you want to live today.

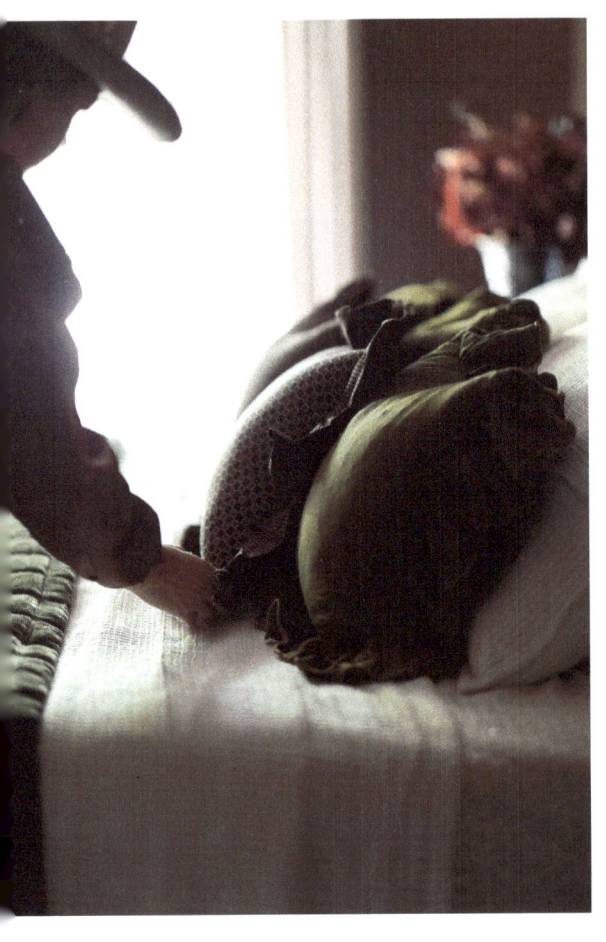

A Quiet Truth I've Carried Since Childhood

When I was ten, my family was quietly unraveling behind the scenes—arguments I didn't understand, tension I couldn't name. My escape was a small closet that became my sanctuary. I lined the floor with soft blankets, taped magazine cut-outs of fashion icons and actresses to the walls, and pressed glow-in-the-dark stars along the baseboards and up the adjoining walls beneath the hanging clothes. Inside that tiny space, the noise faded. It was warm, orderly, and mine.

Looking back, that closet was my first act of design—a child's way of building safety through beauty and order. I didn't know it then, but creating that little world taught me the same lesson I now teach through *Simplified Living*: when your surroundings support you, you can breathe again.

Permission to Keep What Matters

One of the biggest misconceptions about simplifying is that it's about throwing everything away. That's minimalism at its most extreme—and it's not our philosophy.

Simplified Living is about living with enough. Enough to support your daily routines. Enough to reflect your personality and values. Enough to bring joy and function without weighing you down.

This Means You Have Permission to:

- ❖ **Keep what fits your life now.** That could be a bookshelf full of cookbooks you actually use or an oversized sofa perfect for family movie nights.

- ❖ **Hold onto what connects you.** Your grandmother's quilt, the baby blanket you rocked your child in, or a single shoebox of mementos.

- ❖ **Release what drains you.** The jeans that haven't fit in years, the duplicate gadgets, the boxes of "someday projects" you feel guilty about.

Giving yourself this permission takes away the pressure. You don't need to prove you're disciplined enough to live with nothing. You just need to be intentional enough to live with what matters.

Releasing Guilt

If permission is step one, releasing guilt is step two. For many of us, guilt is the biggest barrier to simplifying.

"I paid good money for this—I should use it."

"My friend gave this to me—I'd feel terrible getting rid of it."

"I don't even like it, but I should keep it just in case."

The truth is, the purpose of an item isn't permanent. A gift fulfilled its purpose when it was given with love. A purchase taught you something about your style or needs, even if it turned out to be a mistake. A keepsake holds meaning because of the memory it represents—not because of the object itself.

Releasing guilt means releasing the story that you owe space in your home to anything or anyone. Your home is not a storage unit for other people's expectations. It's the place where your life unfolds now.

Reframing Possessions

What if you began to see your things not as proof of who you are, but as tools that support how you live?

When you reframe possessions this way, you realize:

- ❖ Memories live in you, not in objects.
- ❖ Meaning comes from use, not from storage.
- ❖ Value comes from how something supports your life today.

Your home is not a storage unit for other people's expectations. It's the place where your life unfolds now.

This shift is powerful. Instead of approaching your home with a sense of loss—*What will I have to give up?* You'll approach it with a sense of purpose—*What will I make room for?*

Ways to Bee-gin

- One-In, One-Out: for every new item, something else goes.
- The Reset Routine: spend ten minutes each night putting things back in place.
- The Pre-Purchase Pause: before buying, ask: *Does this serve me now?*
- The Permission Slip: when guilt rises, remind yourself: *I am allowed to let this go.*

Hive Hint

Small steps like these build momentum. Over time, they create a home that naturally stays simpler, lighter, and easier to manage.

A Note on Letting Go

Simplifying isn't about deprivation or perfection—it's about peace. It's about creating a home that feels like a sanctuary, not a storage unit. When you release guilt, honor what matters, and shift your mindset around possessions, you make space not just in your rooms, but in your life.

I know this firsthand. For years, I held onto boxes of gear and keepsakes from my time playing college softball: cleats, jerseys, stacks of tournament T-shirts—things that once represented some of my proudest moments. I thought if I let them go, I'd lose a part of that identity. But what I realized was this: the lessons, the friendships, the grit it taught me—they weren't in the objects. They were in me.

I kept one jersey and my favorite team picture, and I let the rest go. The relief was surprising, almost like stepping back onto the field for a deep, grounding breath. Letting go didn't erase those memories; it made space for me to honor them while fully living the life I have now.

That's the gift of *Simplified Living*. Less isn't about lacking. It's about finally having enough—and trusting that who you are, and the life you're creating, matters more than what sits in a box.

Design Tip

Create one intentional "memory spot"—a single shelf, gallery wall, or keepsake box—so your home reflects your story without overwhelming you.

Nature Note

Just as rivers flow forward, not backward, let go of items that belong to past seasons of life.

The Six-Week Simplify Challenge

The Six-Week Simplify Challenge
A Fresh Start

Maybe you're wondering if this challenge is for you. You might feel the weight of clutter pressing in, or maybe you just know your space isn't working the way it should. If any of these sound familiar, this six-week journey was designed with you in mind:

- ❖ You crave a fresh start in your home and life.
- ❖ You're in transition, newly married, recently graduated, an empty-nester, or downsizing.
- ❖ You've felt overwhelmed by too much stuff and paralyzed about where to begin.
- ❖ You've wasted time looking for lost items (or repurchasing what you already had).
- ❖ Clutter disrupts your focus, your rest, or your ability to enjoy your home.
- ❖ You long for change but feel stuck in the "someday."

If you nodded along to any of those, this challenge is for you.

What You'll Gain:

Simplifying isn't just tidying. It's a transformation. By the end of these six weeks, I hope that you'll feel:

Clarity—knowing where things live; no more frantic searches.

Lightness—the exhale that comes when you let go of excess.

Flow—a home that supports your rhythms instead of fighting them.

Confidence—the strength to keep only what serves you and say goodbye to the rest.

Community—the reminder that you're not alone in this; countless others are on the same journey.

Fun Fact

The Roller-Skating Teacher

Back in high school, my anatomy teacher, Mr. Shoemaker, had a way of making even failure unforgettable. Picture this: bell-bottoms, plaid shirts, curly hair bouncing, and yes—roller skates gliding through the aisles. After handing back tests full of red Xs, he'd call out, "No matter what, YOU are eggs-cellent!" At the time, I rolled my eyes. Looking back, I realize he was teaching us something bigger than anatomy: the power of reframing.

That same mindset applies here. Simplifying can feel like failure—*Why couldn't I keep up? Why did I let things pile up?* But when you reframe, you see it differently: you're not failing, you're learning. You're choosing growth.

Your Simplify Toolkit

Ready to shed the excess and embrace a home that feels lighter, calmer, and more intentional? Before you begin, here's your must-have toolkit to make the process smoother (and even enjoyable):

Cardboard Boxes or Clear Bins—perfect for sorting items into keep, donate, and why-did-I-even-have-this piles.

Trash Bags—some things have served their purpose. Time to say, "Buzz on, Baby!"

Labels & Markers—because "Miscellaneous" is not a category that sparks joy (or helps the future you find anything).

Checklist—track your progress and enjoy those dopamine hits every time you check off a task!

Camera—snap before-and-after photos to see just how far you've come—and for those "Did I really keep this?!" moments.

Epic Playlist—simplifying is way more fun when you're dancing through it. Highly recommended!

Snacks & Beverages—hydrate, caffeinate, and refuel. Simplifying takes energy!

Comfy Clothes—forget the fancy attire—this is a get-your-hands-dirty kind of job.

Headphones—drown out distractions (or unsolicited advice from family about what you should keep).

Determination—because sometimes, letting go is harder than holding onto that 1989 New Kids on the Block concert T-shirt.

Gather your supplies, take a deep breath, and let's clear the clutter—maybe even with a little dance break along the way!

Understanding the Simplified Living Method

Before we dive into Week 1, let's take a moment to understand *The Simplified Living Method*, the structured approach we'll use throughout this journey. Simplifying isn't just about removing things—it's about creating a balanced, functional, and inspiring environment.

The Simplified Living Method Consists of Three Essential Steps:

Simplify: Remove what no longer serves a purpose in your life. This step is all about letting go of excess, whether it's physical clutter, outdated commitments, or mental distractions.

Organize: Create functional systems to maintain order. Once you've cleared the clutter, organization helps ensure that everything has a designated space, making your home easier to manage.

Style: Design a space that inspires and reflects your personality. This final step is where you make your space truly yours—adding meaningful decor, thoughtful arrangements, and personal touches that create a home you love.

A Note on Mindset

This isn't about perfection or staging a magazine-ready house. It's about creating a home that supports you—your routines, your story, and your life as it is right now. The six-week challenge is a roadmap, but it's flexible: go at your pace, pause when you need to, keep what matters, and release the rest. Simplifying isn't just about removing things; it's about curating a life of enough—enough function, enough beauty, enough peace. You're not just organizing your home; you're designing a foundation for the life you want to live. Now, let's begin.

Design Tip

Snap before-and-after photos to see your progress. The visual contrast reinforces motivation and shows how design choices shift energy.

Simplifying isn't about perfection—it's about creating a home that supports your story.

Nature Note

Approach this challenge like planting a garden: steady, daily effort creates beauty and growth over time.

Reflection Questions

Which of the challenge questions at the start of this chapter resonated with you most, and why?

What do you hope to gain—emotionally, mentally, or practically—by committing to this six-week journey?

How do you want your home to feel when you walk through it six weeks from now?

What fears or hesitations do you have about simplifying, and how can you remind yourself that progress is more important than perfection?

Week 1:

The Foundation of Simplifying

The Foundation of Simplifying

Simplifying can feel overwhelming. Maybe you've tried before, only to get stuck halfway through. Perhaps you feel guilty letting go of things, or you're paralyzed by the sheer amount of stuff you've accumulated over the years. You're not alone—simplifying is emotional, but it's also one of the most powerful steps toward clarity and peace.

This week, we'll lay the foundation for your simplifying journey. Simplifying your life isn't just about owning less; it's about shifting your mindset, making intentional choices, and creating a home that truly serves you. Think of this as planting seeds. The small habits and changes you begin now will take root and grow, carrying you through the rest of the challenge, one day at a time.

By the end of this week, you'll have a clear plan, steady motivation, and meaningful progress toward a lighter home and life.

Bee-Inspired: The Hivehouse Co. Approach to Simplifying

At Hivehouse Co., we believe minimalism isn't about deprivation—it's about freedom. Freedom from distractions, from obligations, and from the clutter that keeps you stuck. Simplifying is about being intentional with what you allow into your home and making sure it serves your life with purpose or joy.

This process isn't just about tidying—it's about alignment. When your surroundings reflect your values, you create space for connection, peace, and growth. And just like nature reminds us, there's a season for holding on and a season for letting go. Simplifying is your opportunity to release what no longer brings life so that renewal can take root.

Different Types of Simplifying

Physical Simplifying—releasing items that no longer serve. Clothes, paperwork, kitchen gadgets, or sentimental pieces that carry more weight than joy.

Schedule Simplifying—saying "no" to obligations that don't align with your priorities. Creating margin for what matters most.

Digital Simplifying—organizing files, reducing screen time, clearing emails, and setting boundaries with social media.

Mental Simplifying—letting go of emotional baggage, reducing decision fatigue, and choosing peace over pressure.

In this challenge, we'll focus on physical clutter first. It's the most tangible and gives you quick wins you can see and feel. Clearing what's around you lays the foundation for everything else to follow.

As you simplify, ask yourself:

❖ *Does this serve a real purpose in my daily life?*

❖ *Does it bring me happiness or meaning?*

❖ *If I were shopping today, would I buy this again?*

The goal isn't an empty house. It's a home that supports your rhythms, your relationships, and your growth—without distractions getting in the way.

Simplifying is emotional, but it's also one of the most powerful steps toward clarity and peace.

Hive Tips: Simplifying Your Life Begins with You

The mindset you bring to simplifying matters just as much as the boxes and bins you use. Each choice you make—what to keep, what to release, how to style—carries emotion. These practices help prepare your mind and your home, making the process smoother and more meaningful.

Power Hour: Start with Intention

Give yourself the gift of one quiet hour each morning. Journal, meditate, read, or simply sit in stillness. This is where you release yesterday's clutter from your mind and make room for today. Before you finish, close your eyes and picture your ideal space—how does it look, how does it feel? That vision becomes your permission slip to keep what matters and let go of the rest.

Box & Bin Setup: Sort with Purpose

The right tools make hard decisions easier. Label bins *keep, donate,* and *sell*, along with trash bags for items that have reached the end of their purpose. As you sort, remember: letting go doesn't erase a memory—it frees you to honor it without being buried by it.

Designate a Holding Area

Once something is out of rotation, don't let guilt pull it back in. Choose a spot—a hallway, a garage corner, or a guest room—as a temporary resting place for donations and sales. This physical separation helps your mind release its hold.

Find an Accountabili-Buddy

Simplifying can stir up old emotions. Having a friend, family member, or community to share wins and struggles with makes the process lighter. Say your goals out loud. Share photos. Let connection remind you that you're not doing this alone.

The 15-Minute Timer Rule

Overwhelm thrives on "all or nothing." Instead, set a timer for 15 minutes and tackle one drawer or one shelf. Progress is progress. Like nature, growth comes in steady increments—not all at once. Each small step is proof you're moving forward.

Simplifying isn't a one-time task—it's an ongoing rhythm, like the cycles of nature itself. Release what no longer serves, make space for light and flow, and you'll find clarity unfolding not just in your home, but in every part of your life.

Interactive Action Steps for Week 1

To make this week tangible and productive, follow these structured steps:

Daily Simplifying Task List:

Day 1: Choose a single area (desk, nightstand, junk drawer) and remove anything unnecessary.

Day 2: Start digital simplifying—delete old emails, clear unused apps, and organize files.

Day 3: Tackle one category of items (e.g., books, clothes, kitchen gadgets) and make informed decisions.

Day 4: Review your schedule and commitments—eliminate obligations that don't align with your priorities.

Day 5: Clear a common space (living room, dining table) and experience the clarity it brings.

Day 6: Mindful shopping challenge—avoid unnecessary purchases and reflect on impulse buys.

Day 7: Reflect on your progress—journal about how your space and mindset have shifted.

Before & After Photo Challenge

This first week is about beginning where you are. The photos remind you that progress doesn't have to be dramatic to be meaningful.

Before: Snap a picture of your space exactly as it is—whether it's a messy drawer, a crowded corner, or a cluttered surface.

After: Capture the same spot at the end of the week. Notice the difference in how it looks—and how it feels.

This first reset is proof that even small changes create visible, lasting momentum.

Why This Week Matters

By now, you've taken meaningful steps toward simplifying your space and shifting your mindset. You've begun to clear the excess, create systems, and reshape your environment to support your goals. But the most important takeaway from this week is this: simplifying isn't just about making space—it's about making room for what truly matters in your life.

Design Tip

Before you begin styling, close your eyes and picture your ideal space. Let that vision guide every choice—what stays, what goes, and how the room comes together.

Nature Note

Think of simplifying as planting seeds. Release what no longer serves, make room for light and flow, and let new growth take root.

Reflection Questions

What emotions surfaced as you cleared your first drawer, corner, or surface—relief, hesitation, guilt, or something else?

Which items were the hardest to release, and what story or attachment made them feel that way?

Did you notice a shift in how your space felt once you simplified it? How did that impact your energy or mood?

Looking ahead, what habit or mindset from this week do you want to carry forward into the rest of the challenge?

Honeyed Mindfulness
The Mental Benefits of a Simplified Environment

Simplifying is more than just a physical act—it has profound psychological benefits. When your surroundings are lighter, your mind follows. Simplifying helps by:

- ❖ **Reducing Stress**: fewer visual and mental distractions create calm.

- ❖ **Boosting Energy & Focus:** a clear environment helps you zero in on what matters.

- ❖ **Enhancing Well-being**: a simplified space improves mood and overall satisfaction.

- ❖ **Promoting Freedom**: less stuff means less upkeep and more time for what you love.

- ❖ **Encourages Mindfulness**: living with enough fosters appreciation for what you already have.

Week 1 is about shifting your perspective—learning that less is more and that simplifying isn't about sacrifice but about gaining control over your space and life.

Now that the foundation is set, get ready for Week 2, where we'll take simplifying room by room—starting with the living room, the heart of your hive.

Week 2:

Living Rooms

Living Rooms

The living room is the heart of your hive—a place to gather, unwind, and connect. Because it's the central hub, clutter builds quickly: scattered remotes, unread magazines, extra pillows, and knick-knacks that pile up over time. When this space feels chaotic, it's harder to relax or fully enjoy it.

This week, we'll bring intention and clarity to the living room—reclaiming it as a calm, inviting space that reflects what matters most to you. With clear steps and intentional daily choices, you can reset the energy of this central hub, making it feel lighter, more functional, and easier to maintain.

By the end of the week, the change won't just be something you see—it will be something you feel every time you walk into the room.

Bee-Inspired: The Hivehouse Co. Approach to the Living Room

The living room should invite connection and calm. But when clutter crowds the surfaces and furniture, it works against you instead of for you. *The Simplified Living Method* helps bring it back into balance.

Simplify: Remove what no longer serves a purpose in this space.

Organize: Create simple systems that make daily life easier.

Style: Add intentional touches that reflect your story and make the room welcoming.

Simplifying isn't just about removing objects—it's about shifting your mindset. This room carries layers of emotion: guilt about unused gifts, nostalgia for old keepsakes, or fear of letting go. But your living room doesn't need to hold every story. It needs to hold the ones that matter now.

Like nature, balance comes from both release and renewal. A forest floor thrives when it isn't choked by debris. A river flows freely when it isn't blocked. Your living room thrives when it has room to breathe.

Your living room doesn't need to hold every story—just the ones that matter now.

Step 1. Simplify
Clearing the Excess

Before you start, ask yourself these Three Golden Questions to guide your decisions:

1. **Have I used this item in the last six months?** If not, it's time to donate or sell.

2. **Does this belong in the living room, or should it live elsewhere?** If not, relocate it to its proper place.

3. **Is it broken, outdated, or adding more stress than joy?** If it's beyond repair, toss it. If it's fixable but has been sitting untouched for six months, let it go!

Fun Fact

Facebook Marketplace is my JAM!

Think of it as an online garage sale you never knew you needed—and without the early morning hassle. Time and again, it's been my trusty go-to. Whether you're offloading a bulky couch or searching for a stylish ottoman, there's always someone looking for exactly what you have—or vice versa!

Key Principle: Less Is More

When every surface is crowded, your eye doesn't know where to land—and your mind feels the same. Instead of scattering frames and trinkets across tables, choose a few pieces that truly matter. Curate them into a gallery wall or a single display that tells your story without overwhelming the room. Let open space be part of the design. Fewer, more meaningful items not only look better, but they also make cleaning and upkeep easier.

Simplifying Action Steps:

- ❖ Remove decor that clutters surfaces: keep only what's meaningful or functional.

- ❖ Sort through books, magazines, and decorative items: keep what you love, donate the rest.

- ❖ Reassess furniture: remove oversized or out-of-place items.

- ❖ Gather remotes, cables, and electronics: recycle what's outdated, corral the rest in labeled bins.

- ❖ Create a holding area: corral donations and sales here so they leave the room right away.

Step 2. Organize
Creating Functional Systems

Once the clutter is gone, it's time to establish order so your space stays functional.

Communal Hive: Purpose-Driven Spaces

Decide what your common areas mean to you. What purpose do they serve? Before organizing, define what it is you want your living room to be used for. Is it primarily for:

- ❖ Movie nights?
- ❖ Family game nights?
- ❖ A cozy reading nook?

Once you determine its purpose, everything in the space should align with that function.

Key Principle: Find the Right Fit (& Function)

Your furniture should do more than just fill a room—it should work for your space and your lifestyle. Oversized, outdated pieces can make a room feel cramped and cluttered, while well-chosen furniture enhances both flow and function. If a bulky couch no longer fits your vision, tell it to, "Buzz on, Baby!"

Instead, opt for multi-functional furniture that maximizes space without sacrificing style. Think chic ottomans with hidden storage, coffee tables with built-in organization, or modular seating that adapts to your needs. Simplifying doesn't mean draining your wallet—great secondhand finds on Facebook Marketplace or local shops can help you upgrade your space without breaking the bank.

Organizing Action Steps:

- ❖ Identify clutter-prone areas (side tables, entertainment centers, baskets, etc.)
- ❖ Temporarily remove everything from these areas and clean the surfaces.
- ❖ Sort items into Keep, Donate, or Sell piles.
- ❖ Store frequently used items in accessible spaces (e.g., remotes in a stylish tray).
- ❖ Keep less-used items out of sight—like board games stored in dual-purpose ottomans.
- ❖ Invest in functional furniture with hidden storage to keep clutter at bay.

Hive Hint

If you struggle to keep things tidy, try the "One-Minute Rule"—if something takes less than a minute to put away, do it immediately!

Step 3. Style
Elevating the Space

Styling is where your choices tell the story. It's not about adding more; it's about curating with intention. Texture, light, and layout all shape how people feel in the space.

Key Principle: Room to Breathe (& Connect)

How you arrange your furniture influences both the feel and function of your living room. A thoughtful layout fosters conversation and connection, while a poorly arranged space can make a room—and the people in it—feel disconnected. Avoid common pitfalls like pushing everything against the walls, blocking key focal points like a fireplace, or positioning all seating toward the TV. Instead, create a balanced, inviting arrangement that encourages both movement and interaction.

Styling Action Steps:

- ❖ Sketch a rough layout of the room before moving furniture.
- ❖ Arrange seating around a focal point: fireplaces, coffee tables, or statement art.
- ❖ Call in some backup when it's time to move furniture around: the ideal excuse for a fun evening with your favorite bestie or a loved one.
- ❖ Add a pop of life with a beautiful candle or a decorative plant.
- ❖ Use layered lighting: overhead lights, table lamps, and candles create ambiance.
- ❖ Select aesthetic storage solutions: woven baskets and decorative boxes provide a clutter-free look.
- ❖ Limit decor to a few meaningful pieces: a curated gallery wall, a statement rug, or a sleek coffee table book.

Refresh the space with small swaps—such as pillows, blankets, or rearranging a shelf. Even subtle changes renew the space.

Interactive Action Steps for Week 2

To make this week tangible and productive, follow these structured steps:

Daily Simplifying Task List:

Day 1: Simplify coffee tables, end tables, and entertainment centers.

Day 2: Sort through books, magazines, and decorative items.

Day 3: Organize electronics, cables, and remote controls.

Day 4: Reassess furniture placement and create intentional seating areas.

Day 5: Implement a designated storage system for frequently used items.

Day 6: Add final decorative touches to enhance the room's warmth and style.

Day 7: Reflect on your progress—journal about how your space and mindset have shifted.

Before & After Photo Challenge

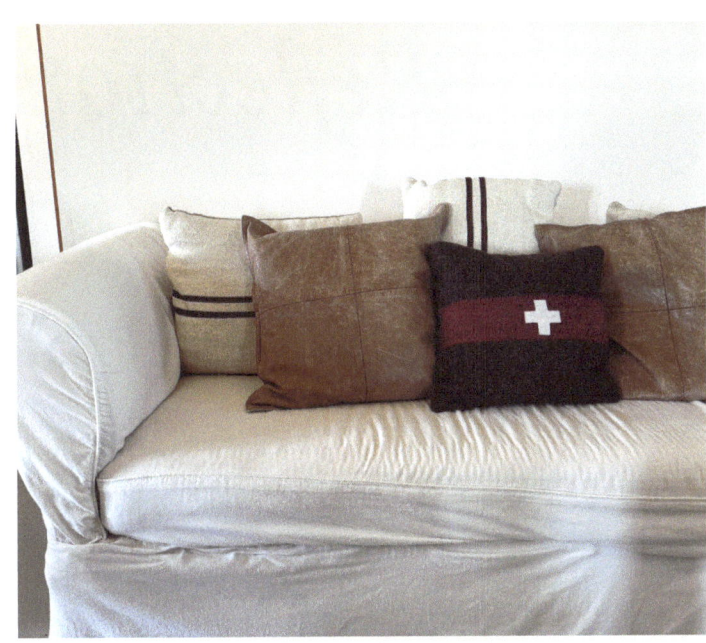

The living room is the heart of your home—so let your photos capture the shift from busy and cluttered to calm and connected.

Before: Take a photo of your living room "as lived in"—piles on the coffee table, extra pillows, or a shelf that's collected more than it should.

After: Photograph the room once it's simplified, organized, and styled. Look for the shift: more space to breathe, more calm when you walk in.

This is the heart of your hive—see how intention changes everything.

Design Tip

Define the purpose of your living room before you organize it. Every item and every piece of furniture should earn its place by supporting that vision.

Nature Note

Trees don't keep every leaf; they let go to make space for new growth. Your living room deserves the same rhythm of release and renewal.

Reflection Questions

When you walk into your simplified living room, how does the energy of the space feel compared to what it was like before?

What items did you choose to keep on display, and what story do they tell about you and your family?

Did letting go of decor or furniture bring up any guilt? How did you move through it?

How has simplifying this shared space affected the way you connect with others in it?

Why This Week Matters

The living room is the heart of your home, but when clutter takes over, it can quickly become a source of stress rather than a source of comfort. Remember, simplifying isn't just about tidying up; it's about making your home work for you and establishing sustainable habits that prevent clutter from creeping back in.

To maintain a clutter-free space in the long term, adopt simple daily habits, such as resetting the room each evening, limiting surface clutter, and practicing mindful purchasing. Small, consistent actions will reinforce the progress you've made, ensuring your living room remains a functional and beautiful space for years to come.

This week's work will set the foundation for maintaining a functional and beautiful space, proving that a clutter-free home isn't just a dream—it's a lifestyle shift that enhances your well-being.

Enjoy your revitalized living room! Take a moment to soak it all in. You did this. Now, grab your favorite drink, kick back, and enjoy the space you've reclaimed. Next up—Week 3: Personal Spaces.

Week 3:

Personal Spaces

Personal Spaces

Our bedrooms, bathrooms, and closets are often the most personal places in our homes—spaces where we start and end our days, unwind, reflect, and regroup. But when clothing spills out of drawers, surfaces collect forgotten odds and ends, and closets turn into chaotic catch-alls, that sense of sanctuary fades.

This week is your invitation to restore order and serenity to these spaces—so they feel like retreats instead of stress zones. We'll bring intention andclarity to your bedrooms, bathrooms, and closets, transforming them into calm, functional spaces that support your routines and reflect your unique style. With each small step, you'll create not only order but also a sense of peace that carries into the rest of your home.

By the end of the week, your bedrooms, bathrooms, and closets will feel more spacious, more "you," and more aligned with the life you're building.

Bee-Inspired: The Hivehouse Co. Approach to Personal Spaces

Your bedrooms and closets are more than storage—they shape your mindset every day. When clutter builds here, it doesn't just create visual noise; it can disrupt sleep, increase stress, and make even simple routines harder. This week's focus is about more than tidying. It's about creating spaces that support your well-being.

Simplifying personal spaces can be emotional. Bedrooms often hold keepsakes, and closets hold "someday" clothes. Releasing guilt, giving yourself permission to keep what truly matters, and letting go of what no longer fits your life are essential steps to take. When you clear away the excess, you open space for rest, clarity, and intention.

We'll move through three meaningful steps:

> **Simplify:** Let go of the excess to create space for calm and renewal.
>
> **Organize:** Set up systems that simplify your day and support your routines.
>
> **Style:** Add cozy, calming elements that personalize your space and promote peace.

This week is your chance to bring intention to the spaces that shape your days—so they not only function smoothly but also reflect who you are and how you want to live. The goal is balance: room to breathe, a few meaningful anchors, and space for life to unfold with ease.

Step 1. Simplify
Clearing the Clutter from Your Cozy Comb

Let's begin with your bedrooms—the space meant for rest and renewal. Take a quick inventory and ask yourself: *Does this belong here, or has it wandered in from somewhere else?* Removing what's out of place instantly clears visual clutter and sets the tone for calm.

Key Principle: Tidy Room, Tidy Mind

A made bed and a clear floor do more for your mindset than you might think. Start your day with these small wins, and you'll carry that sense of order into everything else.

Simplifying Action Steps:

- ❖ Scan the room and identify anything that feels out of place or doesn't belong in the bedroom.

- ❖ Relocate misplaced items to their proper rooms: keep only what supports rest and function.

- ❖ Clear surfaces like nightstands and dressers: limit decor to a few calming, intentional pieces.

- ❖ Reset the space each morning by making the bed and putting away anything left out.

- ❖ Create a designated spot for items to keep, donate, or sell elsewhere in the house.

Step 2. Organize
Creating Flow & Function

Furniture placement and storage shape how your bedroom feels and how easy it is to keep up. A thoughtful layout helps routines flow instead of frustrate.

Key Principle: Find the Flow

The layout of your bedroom directly shapes how comfortable and restful it feels. Thoughtful furniture placement makes daily routines—getting dressed in the morning, winding down at night—smoother and less stressful. Step back and notice how you move through the space. Are pathways clear? Can you easily reach your closet, nightstand, or dresser? If a piece feels bulky, blocks movement, or collects clutter, it may be disrupting the natural flow. Reposition the bed for a better view, swap a large dresser for a smaller one, or remove unnecessary furniture. The goal isn't perfection—it's ease, clarity, and a sense of spaciousness that supports your life.

Bedroom Layout Tips:

- ❖ Assess your current furniture arrangement: does it support flow or feel cramped?

- ❖ Rearrange for easy movement: pieces should be functional and not block natural paths.

- ❖ Place furniture thoughtfully: dressers near closets and nightstands beside the bed.

Closet Calm: Edit with Purpose, Dress with Ease

Closets often hold more than clothes—they hold guilt, nostalgia, or indecision. Outfits saved for "maybe," jeans that don't fit, shoes you never wear. Over time, these items weigh you down.

A simplified closet should feel like a personal wardrobe studio—filled only with pieces that fit, flatter, and feel like you in this season of life.

Closet Action Steps:

- ❖ Choose matching hangers to create visual consistency and save space: uniformity helps your closet feel instantly calmer.

- ❖ Sort items by category (e.g., tops, pants, or occasion) or color to simplify your dressing routine.

- ❖ Use labeled bins or baskets for accessories, off-season items, or shoes: place them onto high shelves or into unused corners.

- ❖ Add shelf dividers to prevent stacks of clothes from toppling or blending together.

- ❖ Store rarely used or sentimental items in clear containers so you can see what's inside without rummaging.

- ❖ Keep a donation bag or bin inside your closet so when you try something on and realize you're done with it, you can easily let it go.

Key Principle: Dress Your Space with Intention

Your closet should support you every morning, not remind you of who you used to be. Keep what connects to the life you're living now, and release the rest.

Organizing Action Steps:

- ❖ Choose low-profile storage bins that fit neatly under your bed: maximize hidden space without adding clutter.

- ❖ Label each container clearly so seasonal or infrequently used items are easy to find when needed.

- ❖ Install wall-mounted shelves in small or teen bedrooms: free up floor space and reduce surface clutter.

- ❖ Group similar items together on shelves: use baskets or bins to keep smaller essentials tidy and accessible.

Step 3. Style
Bringing Personality & Peace to Your Space

Styling is where function meets feeling—and where your story comes through. Once your bedroom is simplified and organized, this step makes it yours. It's not about adding more, but about choosing what feels restful and true to you in this season. Cozy textures, calming colors, soft lighting, or a few meaningful keepsakes can transform a functional room into a retreat that reflects who you are and how you want to feel. The goal is simple: a bedroom that recharges you—mind, body, and spirit.

Key Principle: Curate Your Calm

Your bedroom should feel like a breath of fresh air—not a storage space for everything you've ever owned. Let your favorite pieces shine by giving them space to be seen and appreciated, not lost in visual noise. Display the meaningful. Store the rest with care.

Styling Action Steps:

- ❖ Take photos of your room from different angles to get a fresh perspective. What feels serene and what feels overwhelming?

- ❖ Swap bold patterns or bright colors for neutral, calming tones that support relaxation.

- ❖ Incorporate elements that soothe you: soft lighting, a diffuser with your favorite scent, serene artwork, or a plush rug underfoot.

- ❖ Add small luxuries that invite rest: a weighted blanket, a comfy reading chair, or a sound machine for better sleep.

- ❖ Thoughtfully reflect on keepsakes like jewelry, books, or sentimental items: keep only those that hold meaning in your life today.

- ❖ Curate keepsakes with care: display what has meaning, store the rest with intention.

 *Hive Hint*

Everything you keep should earn its place by bringing peace, not pressure.

From Bedrooms to Bathrooms

Bathrooms may be among the smallest rooms in your home, but they carry enormous influence. They're where mornings begin, evenings wind down, and self-care rituals take place. Yet these spaces often become cluttered catch-alls—counters crowded with products, drawers stuffed with trial sizes, and cabinets hiding more expired products than useful ones. The good news is that small changes in this space ripple outward, shifting the tone of your whole routine.

A bathroom should feel like a retreat, not a storage closet. The goal here is to clear away what's expired, broken, or duplicated, then rebuild the space so it supports daily routines with ease. A few intentional touches—soft towels, natural light, a favorite scent—turn the ordinary into something restorative.

We'll move through three steps:

Simplify: Remove expired, broken, or duplicate products and linens.

Organize: Create functional zones for daily routines and backstock.

Style: Add calming, spa-like touches that bring peace.

Step 1. Simplify
Clear the Counters & Cabinets

Bathroom clutter has a way of sneaking in. Samples accumulate, products multiply, and worn-out towels linger long past their use. Start fresh by emptying every drawer, shelf, and cabinet. Lay it all out where you can see it, group similar items together, and check for what's expired or no longer worth keeping. Release the extras, keep the essentials.

Key Principle: Clarity Creates Calm

A pared-down bathroom immediately feels lighter and more usable.

Simplifying Action Steps:

- ❖ Empty drawers and cabinets: lay everything out where you can see it.
- ❖ Toss expired products, medications, or makeup.
- ❖ Remove duplicates: keep only your go-to favorites; donate unopened extras.
- ❖ Refresh linens: save the best, let go of the rest.
- ❖ Edit your shower: limit to essentials plus one or two favorites.

Step 2. Organize Systems That Support Daily Flow

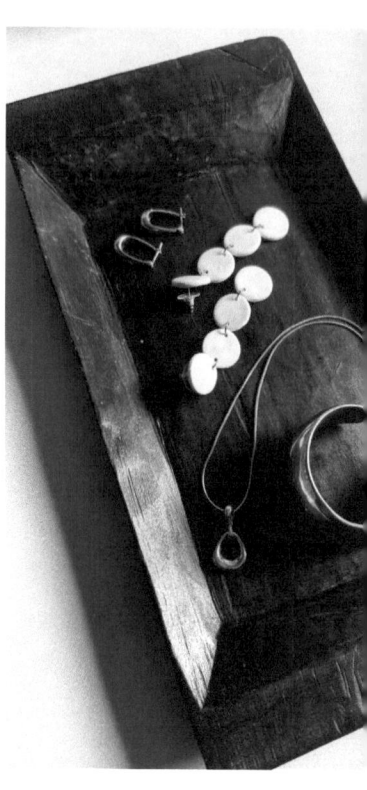

With the excess gone, rebuild your bathroom so it supports—not hinders—your routines. Zones matter: keep daily essentials within reach, and store extras in clear bins for easy restock.

Organizing Action Steps:

- ❖ Countertop corral: use a tray or matching jars to keep the countertop neat.

- ❖ Drawer dividers: separate makeup, grooming tools, and small items.

- ❖ Cabinet categories: sort items by category, such as, skincare, haircare, first aid, and travel sizes.

- ❖ Backstock bins: label bins for refills (soap, toothpaste, toilet paper).

Key Principle: Ease in the Everyday

When everything has a place, mornings move faster and evenings wind down without friction.

Eco-Pollination: Sustainable Swaps

- Switch to refillable soap dispensers or bulk buys to reduce waste.
- Replace single-use wipes or cotton rounds with washable versions.
- Use eco-friendly cleaners and natural scents to keep the space fresh without harsh chemicals.

Step 3. Style
Spa-Like Touches at Home

Bathrooms should restore you, not overwhelm you. When the space is pared back and free of clutter, it opens up room for calm. The atmosphere shifts—steam rising in the quiet, the glow of warm light, the pause of breath as you settle into a slower rhythm.

A well-tended bathroom turns the ordinary acts of washing your face or stepping into the shower into rituals that ground and renew you, reminding you that even the smallest spaces can hold peace.

To maintain the calm you've created, commit to small habits.

Key Principle: Beauty That Restores

Every choice should make the space more soothing and supportive. Choose details that make you exhale.

Styling Action Steps:

- ❖ Layer lighting: bright, clear task lighting for mornings; softer, warmer light for evenings.

- ❖ Add greenery: eucalyptus in the shower, a small potted plant, or fresh flowers bring life to the space.

- ❖ Elevate basics: choose beautiful, refillable dispensers, jars, or containers for everyday items.

- ❖ Introduce calming scents: candles, essential oils, or bath salts. (I love using Himalayan sea salt in a simple stone container—it feels both grounding and elegant.)

Interactive Action Steps for Week 3

To make this week tangible and productive, follow these structured steps:

Daily Simplifying Task List:

Day 1: Take inventory of your bedroom, closet, and bathroom. Return anything that doesn't belong.

Day 2: Clear surfaces—nightstands, dressers, counters. Keep only what you use or what calms you.

Day 3: Rearrange for flow. In the bedroom, shift furniture for easier movement. In the bathroom, create space around the vanity.

Day 4: Simplify your closet. Empty it fully, clean as you go, and notice what no longer fits your life.

Day 5: Sort clothing by category or season. Do the same with bathroom products—group like with like.

Day 6: Mindfully display keepsakes, linens, or toiletries that you've chosen to keep. Let the meaningful pieces stand out.

Day 7: Refresh your space with soft neutrals, clear surfaces, and a small calming detail that makes it feel like yours again.

Before & After Photo Challenge

Bedrooms, closets, and bathrooms all set the tone for how you live. The images this week will show how much lighter life feels when these spaces support you.

Before: Capture your bedroom, bathroom or closet before the reset—an unmade bed, a crowded vanity, a closet that feels too heavy.

After: Take the same photo once it's simplified. Notice the lighter surfaces, the clearer flow, and how the room feels when it supports you instead of drains you. This is where your hive's routines are created—see how intention changes everything.

These are the rooms that hold your energy, let them return it to you.

Design Tip

Choose consistency in your closet—matching hangers, simple bins, or uniform dividers. Visual order creates instant calm and makes getting dressed feel effortless.

Nature Note

Clear space invites calm. Just as light moves more freely through an open window, your bedroom feels more restful when surfaces and floors aren't crowded.

Reflection Questions

What emotions came up while editing your closet—did you feel tied to old versions of yourself, or did you feel free to embrace who you are now?

How did simplifying your bedrooms or bathrooms shift the way you begin and end your days?

Where do you feel the biggest difference—in rest, in routines, or in peace of mind?

What new habit will help you keep these personal spaces steady, calm, and supportive going forward?

Why This Week Matters

Bedrooms, closets, and bathrooms hold more influence than their size suggests. They're the spaces where you pause, prepare, and return to yourself. When they're crowded or neglected, the weight shows up in your day; when they're clear and intentional, they give back a sense of calm.

This week wasn't just about tidying drawers or folding towels. It was about creating spaces that reflect your needs right now, support your routines, and return calm to the moments that matter most.

To hold onto that calm, commit to small habits: reset your bed each morning, keep counters and surfaces clear, and edit what comes into these spaces. These consistent choices protect the balance you've built and remind you that your space is meant to support you, not weigh you down.

With your personal spaces refreshed, you're ready to take on Week 4: Work Spaces—where your inner worker bee can shine!

Week 4:

Workspaces

Workspaces

Your home office or study space is the engine room of your hive—the place where ideas take shape, goals are tackled, and checklists finally meet their match. Whether you're managing a household, running a business, balancing remote work, or supporting a student through schoolwork, this space keeps everything in motion. It's where focus takes root and progress unfolds.

But when the surfaces are buried under paperwork, cords are in a tangle, and supplies have no home, it becomes harder to concentrate—let alone feel inspired. Clutter, whether physical or digital, creates mental noise that drains your energy and slows your momentum. Even small tasks start to feel overwhelming when your environment is working against you.

This week is about reclaiming your workspace—whether it's a dedicated office, a makeshift desk in the corner, or a shared study zone used by the whole household. With a few intentional changes, you'll clear distractions, streamline your systems, and create a workspace that supports creativity, focus, and calm—no matter what's on your plate. Let's reset the space where you think, create, and get things done.

A cluttered desk reflects a cluttered mind.

Bee-Inspired: The Hivehouse Co. Approach to Workspaces

Your home office or study space isn't just about efficiency—it's about energy. A cluttered desk reflects a cluttered mind. When digital files, physical papers, and supplies compete for attention, productivity stalls. But when your workspace is aligned with your routines, even the busiest days feel lighter and more manageable.

This week, we'll help you streamline not just your physical desk, but your digital world as well. Because let's be real—a clean desktop matters just as much as a clear desk. Through thoughtful edits and simple upgrades, you'll create a space that fuels clear thinking and steady progress.

Simplify: Remove the excess on your desk, on your screens, and in your drawers.

Organize: Set up smart systems and storage so everything has a purpose and a place.

Style: Add thoughtful design touches that inspire creativity and support focused work.

Let's create a workspace that sparks ideas and keeps you on task—without the constant background buzz of clutter.

Step 1. Simplify
Clear the Chaos to Focus

Whether you work at a desk, a kitchen table, or a cozy corner, the first step is the same: strip it down. Piles of paper, half-used notebooks, and cords snaking everywhere aren't just eyesores—they're friction points that slow you down and steal your focus and energy. The goal this week isn't to create a Pinterest-perfect office—it's to reset your workspace so it works for you.

Key Principle: Clear Space, Clear Mind

Visual noise distracts the brain and drains your energy. A clean, focused environment allows your thoughts to flow and your tasks to follow.

Simplifying Action Steps:

- ❖ Start with a clean slate: clear everything off your desk—yes, every single item.

- ❖ Sort what you removed into categories: office supplies, paperwork, tech accessories, and miscellaneous clutter.

- ❖ Be selective as you return items: only put back what you use regularly and what supports your daily workflow.

- ❖ Untangle and unplug all cords: bundle them neatly using velcro straps, twist ties, or cable clips. Label or discreetly tuck away charging cables, power strips, and excess wires to maintain a clean, streamlined surface.

Step 2. Organize
Set Up for Efficiency

Now that your workspace is cleared, it's time to rebuild with intention and organize it in a way that works for you. Organization isn't just about storage—it's about creating systems that support the way you think, plan, and work. Thoughtful placement and accessible systems reduce friction and help you stay focused.

Desk Dynamics: *Function Meets Focus*

Your desktop is the control center of your workspace. But when it's buried under five mugs, last week's mail, and random supplies, even the simplest tasks can feel like a chore. Think of your desk as prime real estate—only the essentials should live here. Everything else? It belongs in a drawer, a bin, or better yet, out of the way.

Desk Action Steps:

- ❖ Limit your desktop to the essentials: keep only what you use daily, like your laptop, planner, and one or two writing tools.

- ❖ Store small items neatly: use drawer dividers or a desktop caddy to prevent clutter from piling up.

- ❖ Repurpose a container for tools: a decorative mug or cup works perfectly for pens, markers, or scissors.

- ❖ Keep surfaces clear: stow extras in labeled bins or drawers to reduce visual distraction.

- ❖ Control cord chaos: use clips or organizers to keep wires tucked away and untangled.

Workspace Organization: Systems That Stick

Beyond your desk, your entire work zone should be built for efficiency. Systems don't have to be complicated—they just need to be consistent and practical for your everyday routines.

Organizing Action Steps:

- ❖ Group like items together: sort supplies into categories such as writing tools, tech accessories, and paper products.

- ❖ Assign each group a designated home: use labeled containers, baskets, or drawer organizers to keep everything organized and in place.

- ❖ Designate a supply station: from paper clips to Post-its, everything should have a designated spot.

- ❖ Store infrequently used items elsewhere: place them higher up or in closed storage to minimize distraction.

- ❖ Add a recycling bin or tray nearby: having a spot for paper waste helps maintain a clean, functional surface.

Key Principle: Sustainable Systems

The best organizational systems are the ones you'll actually use—simple, sustainable, and tailored to your real-life habits. When everything has a clear home, it's easier to stay on task, keep clutter at bay, and reset your space in minutes—not hours.

Digital Swarm
Clear the Clutter Behind the Screen

It's not just your desk that can spiral into chaos—your digital space can quietly steal your focus, too. Overflowing inboxes, scattered files, and outdated apps may not take up physical space, but they create the same sense of overwhelm and distraction. Clearing your digital clutter is like clearing mental static—it allows you to think more clearly, act more efficiently, and feel more in control of your day.

This step isn't about achieving digital perfection. It's about creating clean, functional digital systems that make your daily work easier and smoother.

Digital Simplifying Action Steps:

Inbox Insight—Filter, File & Free Your Focus

- ❖ Create folders or labels: sort messages into categories like Work, Personal, To-Do, and Reference to streamline your inbox.

- ❖ Set up email filters: automatically route incoming emails to the correct folders so you don't have to sort everything manually.

- ❖ Unsubscribe from the unnecessary: let go of newsletters, promotions, or updates that no longer serve you.

- ❖ Commit to a daily review: spend 15–20 minutes each day archiving or deleting old messages to keep your inbox manageable.

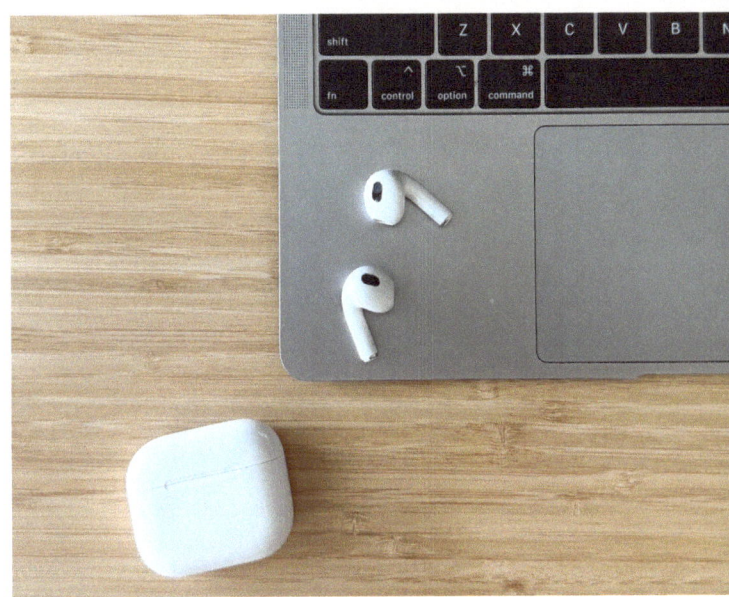

File Finesse—Streamline Storage for Stress-Free Searching

- ❖ Build a logical folder structure: organize files by category, project, or date—whatever makes the most sense for how you work.

- ❖ Delete duplicates and outdated files: clear the digital noise to improve both focus and device performance.

- ❖ Rename files with clarity: use searchable, descriptive names so you're not stuck guessing what "FinalDraft_v3(2)" means.

- ❖ Back up essential documents: use cloud storage or an external hard drive to ensure your important files are safe and accessible.

Software Scrub—Clean Up, Clear Out & Click with Confidence

- ❖ Review and uninstall unused apps: remove anything you haven't used in the last three to six months to reclaim digital space.

- ❖ Update what matters: ensure key programs and software are running the latest versions for better performance and security.

- ❖ Clear your desktop: remove cluttered shortcuts and random downloads—keep only what you need front and center.

Key Principle: Tidy Tech, Sharper Focus

Digital clutter may be invisible, but its effects are very real. Each time you sift through a chaotic inbox, dig for a lost file, or navigate outdated software, your brain expends energy that could be better spent elsewhere. A streamlined digital environment frees up your mental bandwidth, reduces decision fatigue, and allows you to transition between tasks with greater ease.

Simplifying your tech isn't about perfection—it's about creating intentional digital systems that support your day, rather than disrupting it. When your files are findable, your inbox is manageable, and your tools work seamlessly, your focus sharpens and your productivity naturally follows.

Step 3. Style
Bringing Personality & Peace to Your Space

With your workspace simplified and organized, it's time to give it personality and purpose. Styling isn't about over-decorating or creating something Pinterest-perfect—it's about crafting an environment that supports how you want to feel and function throughout your day. Whether you're aiming for energized focus or peaceful flow, your space should help get you there.

A well-styled workspace doesn't just look better—it works better. Through simple, intentional choices, you can transform a basic setup into a personalized zone that helps you stay grounded, inspired, and ready to take on whatever's ahead.

Key Principle: Make Your Space Work for You

Your workspace should reflect both the work you do and the energy you want to carry while doing it. Everything in your space should either fuel your productivity or nurture your well-being—nothing more, nothing less.

———————— Hive Hint

Zoning is one of the easiest ways to improve the feel and function of your workspace. Think about how you use the space—do you have a spot for focused work, a place to plan, and a corner to breathe or reset?

Styling Action Steps:

- ❖ Create dedicated areas: a desk for focus, a chair or corner for reading, and a shelf for storage or inspiration.

- ❖ Layer your lighting: use natural light whenever possible, and supplement it with warm desk lamps or floor lights for added comfort and visibility.

- ❖ Choose meaningful accessories: keep decor minimal but motivating–think a framed quote, a calming print, or a small plant can go a long way.

- ❖ Prioritize comfort: add elements that support your body, like a cushioned chair, footrest, or ergonomic add-ons for longer work sessions.

- ❖ Incorporate calming scent: use a diffuser, candle, or essential oil roller to signal focus or relaxation, depending on what you need.

- ❖ Add texture and personality: a cozy throw, a soft rug underfoot, or a vision board above your desk can bring warmth and inspiration.

Interactive Action Steps for Week 4

To make this week tangible and productive, follow these structured steps:

Daily Simplifying Task List:

Day 1: Clear your entire workspace and assess what actually belongs.

Day 2: Organize your desk drawers, office supplies, and cords.

Day 3: Create or tidy your supply station with caddies, bins, or pegboards.

Day 4: Tackle your email inbox—set up folders, filters, and unsubscribe.

Day 5: Simplify and organize your digital files and software.

Day 6: Style your workspace with light, scent, and visual clarity.

Day 7: Reflect, fine-tune, and reset for the week ahead.

Before & After Photo Challenge

Your workspace shapes your focus. These photos highlight how clearing surfaces and systems clears your head, too.

Before: Snap your desk or study zone as it is—piles of paper, tangled cords, or a computer desktop that makes you anxious.

After: Take a photo once your workspace is clear, organized, and styled with purpose.

See how a reset environment sharpens your focus and lightens your mental load.

Design Tip

Think zones, not piles. Define where you focus, where you store, and where you reset—even in a small space.

Even small tasks start to feel overwhelming when your environment is working against you.

Nature Note

Light flows best through open space. When your desk is clear, ideas move with the same ease.

Reflection Questions

How did clearing your desk or study zone affect your ability to focus?

Did you notice parallels between physical clutter on your desk and digital clutter on your devices?

Which organizing system feels most natural to you, and why?

What styling choice (lighting, plants, layout) made your workspace feel more supportive of your work or creativity?

Why This Week Matters

Your home office or study space might be small, but its impact on your daily life is significant. A cluttered desk or chaotic inbox can leave you feeling scattered, frustrated, and drained. This week wasn't just about clearing surfaces—it was about creating flow: physically, digitally, and mentally.

What you cleared went beyond piles of paper or tangled cords—it was mental noise, decision fatigue, and invisible distractions. By editing your space and simplifying your digital world, you created room for clarity in how you think, work, and move through your day. Your workspace is no longer something to manage—it's something that supports you.

More than a tidy desk, you've built a space that reflects your rhythm, respects your focus, and honors your energy. Keep the momentum going by resetting daily, refining systems as needed, and checking in with what helps you thrive. Your environment now works with you—not against you—and that shift makes all the difference.

With your workspaces bee-lined for productivity, you're ready to take on Week 5: Kitchens—the busiest zones of your hive!

Week 5:

Kitchens & Storage

Kitchens

The kitchen is more than a room for cooking. It's the fueling station of your hive—the space where meals are made, stories are told, and daily rhythms intersect. But it's also where clutter likes to take root. Counters fill with appliances you rarely touch. Spices often hide in the back of cabinets until they're long past their useful life. Overflow shelves and storage zones turn into limbo for tools, bins, and boxes you've forgotten you even own.

This week is about more than clearing surfaces—it's about restoring flow in the spaces that sustain you. With *The Simplified Living Method*, you'll reimagine your kitchen and storage not just for how they look, but for how they feel, how they function, and what they nourish.

When you pare back to what truly earns its place, cooking becomes less of a scramble and more of a rhythm. Counters stay clear, tools are easy to reach, and systems hold steady, making meals simpler, choices healthier, and connections easier.

The kitchen returns to what it was always meant to be: a place where life slows down, nourishment feels effortless, and gathering together takes center stage.

Rebuild your spaces so they serve you—not the other way around.

Bee-Inspired: The Hivehouse Co. Approach to Kitchens & Storage

Simplified Living isn't just how your home looks—it's how it feels. It's about curating a kitchen that supports your routines, restores your energy, and brings joy to daily rituals.

That might mean tossing expired cans, donating duplicates, and letting go of gadgets that promised to make life easier but ended up in the way. But it also means adding back what truly serves—like fresh herbs within reach, a crock of utensils that are as beautiful as they are useful, or a pantry system that saves time and reduces waste.

Even the simplest reset can change how you move through the day. A bowl of harvested peppers on the counter, a jar of nasturtium blooms brightening your porch, a favorite mug waiting for your morning coffee. *Simplified Living* is about slowing down to notice beauty in the everyday, surrounding yourself with things that do more than decorate—they give back.

This week, we'll move through three steps:

Simplify: Remove expired food, unused appliances, and cluttered storage.

Organize: Create functional zones and sustainable systems that make life easier.

Style: Add touches that invite connection, comfort, and beauty that serve a purpose.

Soon, every cupboard and counter will support easy meals and happy moments, not chaos.

Step 1. Simplify
Counter & Cabinet Clear Out

Counters crowded with unused appliances and shelves stuffed with forgotten cans don't just take up space—they also steal energy and joy from cooking. The remedy is a complete reset: clear every surface, empty each cabinet, and pull out what's been hiding. With everything visible, choose only the tools, ingredients, and containers that make daily prep smoother and mealtimes more enjoyable. Let the rest buzz off to donation, recycling, or the trash.

Key Principle: Clarity for Culinary Ease

When your prep space is clear, your mind follows suit. Open counters mean less visual noise, faster cleanup, and fewer decisions between you and dinner. The clearer your prep zones, the smoother your cooking flow.

Simplifying Action Steps:

- ❖ Sort every utensil: pull them all out, group by type, and ditch duplicates or damaged pieces.

- ❖ Create a discard pile: toss broken tools; donate extras that haven't seen action in months.

- ❖ Define appliances: if they haven't been used in the past year, they're not essential.

- ❖ Date-check pantry and fridge items: toss anything expired and group foods by category.

- ❖ Empty hidden storage: clear closets, garage shelves, or attic boxes to see what's truly worth keeping.

Step 2. Organize
Systems That Nourish

With the excess gone, rebuild your spaces so they serve you—not the other way around. Every item has a place and every space has a purpose, especially in the kitchen. The goal isn't to create a showroom—it's to make your space work as smoothly as possible for the life you're actually living.

Key Principle: Sustainable Systems

The simplest system is the one you'll maintain—labels, clear bins, and logical zones keep clutter from creeping back. Clear categories, visible storage, and simple resets make organization a rhythm instead of a chore.

Pantry Precision

- ❖ Create shelf "departments": snacks, grains, baking, and canned goods each get their own zone.

- ❖ Label clear bins: write contents and expiration dates so everyone can easily identify what's inside.

- ❖ Adopt the FIFO (first-in, first-out) rotation: keeps food fresh and reduces waste.

Countertop Command

- ❖ Keep only daily tools handy: store spatulas and tongs in one crock; everything else goes in drawers.

- ❖ Use drawer dividers: slot utensils by size and purpose to end the "daily dig".

- ❖ Group cooking zones: cutting boards near prep area; pots near the stove for easy grab-and-go.

Eco-Pollination: Reduce Waste, Compost & Recycle

- ❖ Set up a compost corner: choose a bin style, place it outdoors or under the sink, and teach the hive what goes into it.

- ❖ Create a recycling station: separate glass, metal, and paper with labeled bins for easy drop-off.

- ❖ Swap single-use items: replace disposable towels, bags, and bottles with durable, washable alternatives.

Storage Spaces: Garages, Closets & Attics

Out of sight doesn't have to mean out of control. These hidden zones often carry the heaviest emotional weight—where unfinished projects, "someday" items, and family hand-me-downs quietly pile up. With a little structure, garages, closets, and attics can shift from catch-alls into reliable backup zones that save time rather than swallow it. Assign clear zones for tools, seasonal decor, or bulk supplies. Use clear bins, pegboards, and overhead racks to maximize space, and schedule quick reviews so mystery boxes and half-used cans don't pile up unnoticed.

A Note on Garages

For many households, the garage is the hardest space to tackle. It holds memories, tools, and the "I-might-need-this-one-day" boxes that never seem to leave. If yours feels too big to face in one week, start small—one wall, one shelf, one Saturday. Park your car? Maybe not yet. And that's okay. Simplifying the garage could be its own six-week challenge. This week, focus on progress, not perfection.

Organizing Action Steps:

❖ Assign purpose by zone: group shelves by function: everyday dishes, cookware, pantry staples, or serving pieces.

❖ Prioritize placement: keep daily items at eye level, heavier or less-used pieces down low, and special-occasion items higher up.

❖ Use consistent containers: clear bins, turntables, or baskets corral pantry goods, baking supplies, or snacks for quick access.

❖ Label as you go: a simple label makes it easy for anyone to find (and return) items without rummaging.

❖ Maximize depth: install shelf risers, pull-out drawers, or dividers to keep items visible and accessible instead of buried.

❖ Set review points: each season, scan for expired food, chipped dishes, or gadgets you don't use, and let them go.

Step 3. Style
Flavor, Warmth & Welcome

Function makes a kitchen usable, but style makes it a place people want to linger. Design here is more than aesthetics—it's a form of storytelling. Every choice says something about how you want to live and gather. A few intentional touches—light for clarity, texture for comfort, color for personality—can transform routine prep into an experience that feels both grounding and inviting, all without tipping back into clutter.

Key Principle: Style That Serves

Every element you bring into the kitchen should earn its place by making tasks easier or the space more welcoming. Beauty here should always give back: light that clarifies, textures that comfort, aromas that reset your mood. When a kitchen looks good and works well, people naturally gather, conversations flow, and cooking feels less like a chore.

Styling Action Steps

- ❖ Layer task and ambient lighting: under-cabinet LEDs brighten prep areas, while warm pendants or a soft table lamp add evening ambiance.

- ❖ Display attractive essentials: a ceramic crock of wooden spoons or a handsome cutting board keeps tools handy and doubles as decor.

- ❖ Introduce texture and color: a woven runner, small herb plant, or a trio of colorful canisters brings warmth to neutral counters.

- ❖ Create a grab and go snack zone: a simple tray with fresh fruit, nuts, or granola bars encourages healthy bites and keeps the counter tidy.

- ❖ Add a touch of aroma: a stovetop simmer pot, herb bouquet, or discreet diffuser can infuse the space with a welcoming, natural fragrance.

With these subtle upgrades, your kitchen invites connection, sparks creativity, and stays free of visual noise—proving style and function can blend as smoothly as your favorite recipes.

Interactive Action Steps for Week 5

To make this week tangible and productive, follow these structured steps:

Daily Simplifying Task List:

Day 1: Empty utensil drawers and sort—*keep, donate, or sell.*

Day 2: Evaluate appliances—clean, donate, or find them a new home.

Day 3: Clear pantry and fridge—toss expired items, group by category.

Day 4: Organize drawers with dividers—label shelves and bins.

Day 5: Set up compost/recycling stations—swap single-use items.

Day 6: Simplify cabinets—zone by work flow and restock.

Day 7: Style your kitchen—lighting, decor, and a welcoming snack.

Before & After Photo Challenge

The kitchen fuels your body and your hive's daily rhythm. A cluttered counter or overstuffed pantry slows you down and wastes energy—much like expired food wastes resources. By clearing gadgets you don't use, labeling what you keep, and styling with purpose, time at the table feels less rushed and more restorative.

The kitchen sets the rhythm for daily life. Let your photos show how much smoother it feels when prep zones and storage finally work for you.

Before: Photograph your pantry shelves, jammed drawers, or cluttered counters before you dig in.

After: Take the same shot once zones are set, shelves are labeled, and counters are clear.

This is where daily rhythms begin—capture the shift from chaos to flow.

Design Tip

Style your kitchen with utility in mind: a row of hooks for mugs, baskets for produce, or a tray for oils by the stove keeps things functional and beautiful.

Nature Note

Clarity is nourishment—open counters invite energy to flow, just as open soil invites plants to root.

Reflection Questions

What surprised you most about what you found in your kitchen or storage areas—duplicates, expired items, or forgotten tools?

Did simplifying these areas shift the way you approach meal prep or daily routines? How?

How does your kitchen feel now that only the essentials remain?

What system or styling touch (labels, lighting, layout) made the most significant difference in function or flow?

Why This Week Matters

This week wasn't just about wiping shelves or tossing expired jars—it was about reclaiming ease. What you cleared went far beyond dusty gadgets and forgotten cans; it was decision fatigue, wasted minutes, and the frustration of never finding what you needed. By editing your tools, labeling essentials, and adding purposeful style, you've created systems that respect your time, reduce stress, and invite connection.

Your kitchen now fuels you instead of draining you. Storage spaces serve instead of frustrate you. And that shift ripples outward, shaping not just how you cook, but how you gather, share, and live. More than a tidy counter, you've built rhythms that honor your routines, reduce waste, and free energy for what matters most.

Keep the momentum by resetting after each meal, adjusting zones as needs change, and staying mindful of what truly earns a place. Your environment now works with you—not against you—and that shift will flavor every dish you prepare and every moment you gather to enjoy it.

And if the garage—or that closet or attic—still feels like a beast, give yourself grace. Those zones hold years of memories, projects, and "one-day" boxes, and they can take longer to tame. Start small—one shelf, one bin, one Saturday. Progress counts. The goal isn't perfection; it's creating spaces that feel safer, lighter, and easier to navigate.

With your kitchen humming, you're ready for Week 6: Giving Back & Community Swap—sharing the surplus and spreading the Hivehouse Co. spark!

Week 6:

Community & Giving Back

Community & Giving Back

The journey of simplifying doesn't end when your home feels lighter—it continues in how you release what no longer serves you. This week is about giving with intention: turning "stuff I don't need" into resources, opportunities, and joy for someone else. *Simplified Living* reminds us that when we align what we own with what we value, generosity has room to flow. And when we give, we don't lose—we multiply.

What began six weeks ago as an inward reset now expands outward. A bag of clothes, a box of books, or an unused appliance doesn't have to become waste—in the right hands, it can meet a need or spark delight. With thoughtful planning, donation piles become purposeful deliveries, swap meets become connection points, and small acts of generosity ripple through your community long after this week ends.

Bee-Inspired: The Hivehouse Co. Approach to Community Giving

Simplifying has never been about creating emptiness—it's about creating space for what nourishes and allowing the rest to serve a new purpose. Sometimes that means keeping the quilt your grandmother stitched, and sometimes it means releasing a jacket that will keep a neighbor warm. Passing things along extends their story, proving usefulness doesn't end with you.

When you donate quality items, share your skills, or host a neighborhood swap, you strengthen the hive. You save resources, reduce waste, and create opportunities for others—all while enjoying the quiet lift generosity brings. Community giving mirrors nature's rhythm: nothing is wasted, everything cycles back. Just as fallen leaves enrich the soil, what you release can enrich someone else's day, home, or season of life.

This week, we'll explore three steps—not for your drawers or shelves, but for how you release what you've already simplified. The focus here isn't on what stays, but on how what leaves can still add value.

Simplify with Purpose: Instead of tossing items mindlessly into a bag, take the time to match donations with real needs. The right jacket, book, or appliance in the right hands makes all the difference.

Share the Surplus: When neighbors come together to swap, trade, or even sell at a low cost, generosity multiplies. What you no longer use becomes someone else's solution, and a connection grows in the process

Sustain the Hive: *Simplified Living* isn't just a one-time purge. By giving your time, talent, or ongoing support to community organizations, you build rhythms of generosity that last long after the week ends.

Step 1. Simplify with Purpose
Thoughtful Donation

Dropping off a box at the nearest thrift store is a start. But intentional donation goes further. When items are matched with people and organizations that genuinely need them, your clutter becomes care.

Key Principle: Right Item, Right Place

A little research ensures every box you give meets a real need, making the act of donation efficient and meaningful. Don't just give—give well. Thoughtfulness makes generosity last. And here's an added bonus—many charitable donations are tax-deductible. Your generosity can give twice: once to someone in need, and again when it lightens your financial load at year's end.

Responsible Release

Some things can't be donated—but they don't have to be wasted. Explore eco-friendly disposal, recycling, or creative upcycling. A chipped mug might become a planter. A worn T-shirt can be cut into cleaning rags.

Action Steps

- ❖ Compile local options: schools, shelters, food pantries, and nonprofits often publish wish lists.

- ❖ Match needs to items: check each organization's wish list before you pack items to be donated.

- ❖ Refresh before you release: wash, repair, and package with care. A thank-you note tucked inside a box can remind recipients they matter.

- ❖ Schedule and deliver: schedule drop-offs or arrange pickups so bags don't linger in the trunk or garage.

Step 2. Share the Surplus
Swaps & Sales

Generosity isn't only about giving away—it's about creating exchanges where everyone gains. A neighborhood swap, a pay-what-you-can garage sale, or a community "free table" keeps items in circulation while sparking connection.

Hive Hint

Start with $200 in change if selling.

Key Principle: Share the Surplus

When one person's extra becomes another's missing piece, both parties (and the planet) win.

Event Planning Steps

- ❖ Choose the format: free swap, pay-what-you-can, or classic garage sale.

- ❖ Select a space: driveways, church halls, or school gyms make excellent hubs.

- ❖ Pick a date: coordinate with community calendars to avoid or collaborate with other local events.

- ❖ Spread the word: flyers, word of mouth, or a quick social post can gather a crowd.

- ❖ Organize displays: set up tables, group like items, label clearly, and keep walkways clear.

- ❖ Encourage reuse: provide bags, boxes, or baskets for shoppers to carry items home.

When surplus is shared locally, it builds bonds as much as it clears clutter.

Step 3. Sustain the Hive
Partnerships & Volunteering

Generosity doesn't end with a one-time drop-off. It grows stronger when built into your rhythms, just like resetting your counters or making your bed. By partnering with local organizations or offering your skills, you keep the giving cycle alive year-round.

Key Principle: Give Time, Not Just Things

Volunteering skills can be more valuable than any object you donate. Objects meet immediate needs. Skills, presence, and care build lasting impact.

Golden Nectar Rewards: The Rewards of Generosity

When you give, you lighten more than shelves—you lighten your spirit. Neuroscience shows generosity activates reward centers in the brain, but you don't need science to feel it. You know the shift when a bag leaves your car and lands where it's needed. You sense it in the gratitude of neighbors at a swap. You feel it in the clarity of knowing your things have a purpose again.

Partnership & Volunteer Steps:

❖ Identify shared values: partner with groups whose mission aligns with your own.

❖ Offer specific skills: from organizing drives to graphic design, match your talents to a charity's needs.

❖ Commit to rhythm: monthly volunteering or seasonal check-ins build trust and reliability.

❖ Invite others: share your practice of Simplified Living by mentoring friends or family in their own giving cycles and circles.

Interactive Action Steps for Week 6

To make this week tangible and productive, follow these structured steps:

Daily Simplifying Task List:

Day 1: Review donation piles and group them by category (clothes, books, kitchenware, decor, etc.)

Day 2: Match items with a purpose and align each category with an organization that can use it.

Day 3: Prepare donations by washing, mending, and neatly packaging; add labels or a quick thank-you note.

Day 4: Clear donations from your home by scheduling drop-offs or booking pickup appointments.

Day 5: Share surplus locally by setting aside a few items for neighbors, friends, or a small swap with your community.

Day 6: Extend generosity by exploring volunteer opportunities or ways your skills could support a local group.

Day 7: Reflect on what left your home this week, how it feels to release it, and what kind of impact it may carry forward.

Before & After Photo Challenge

This week's transformation is about what leaves your home—and the story it carries. Your photos will show generosity in action.

Before: Snap a photo of your donation piles, the overflowing garage corner, or the boxes waiting by the door.

After: Capture the cleared space once they're gone—or document the drop-off itself.

Generosity has its own kind of beauty—see the difference in both space and spirit.

Design Tip

Don't just box up donations—present them with the same care you'd use in your own home. Fold clothes neatly, bundle books, or add a thank-you note. It turns decluttering into a gift.

Nature Note

Like seeds carried on the wind, what you release today can take root in places you may never see.

> When we give, we don't lose—we multiply.

Reflection Questions

How did it feel to release items knowing they'd be used and appreciated by someone else?

What did you notice about your own mindset as donation piles left your home?

Did giving back shift your understanding of what *Simplified Living* means?

How do you want generosity—whether with time, belongings, or connection—to continue beyond this challenge?

Why This Week Matters

Simplifying began as an inward reset—clearing clutter, releasing guilt, and creating space in your own home. Giving back carries that freedom outward. What you've released becomes someone else's resource, what you've organized ripples into your community, and what you've styled into a story proves that even ordinary objects can connect people in extraordinary ways.

By now, your hive doesn't just feel lighter—it feels linked to something larger. This week, you turned excess into opportunity, reduced waste, and strengthened bonds around you. Your home feels lighter, yes—but so does your spirit.

That's the heart of *Simplified Living*: beauty that gives back, spaces that support life, and rhythms that nourish not just you, but the people you love and the community you share. With this giving cycle in motion, your journey comes full circle. Simplifying isn't the end—it's the foundation for a life that's lighter, more intentional, and open for deeper connections.

Designing with Purpose

Designing with Purpose

Where Form, Function & Feeling Meet

Designing with purpose is where form, function, and feeling finally meet. It's not about chasing trends or achieving perfection—it's about alignment. When a room supports how you live and reflects what you value, it becomes more than pretty; it becomes powerful.

Design isn't just visual—it's experiential. It's the way light shifts across a surface, how a chair welcomes your body, how a shelf holds both a photograph and a memory. A home designed with purpose tells a story: one of your rhythms, your values, and the life you're actively choosing.

The Emotional Side of Design

Too often, we think of design as something surface-level—paint colors, fabric choices, stylish accents. But at its best, design shapes how we feel. A poorly arranged room can stir frustration. A mismatched chair can feel like an interruption every time you sit. A table too crowded for dinner leaves you disconnected, even in the presence of people you love.

When design is intentional, those same spaces flip the script. You sit down and feel supported. You gather and feel connected. You look around and see not just decor, but reminders of who you are and what you value.

Permission to Design with Intention

Simplified Living gives you permission to design for the life you're living now, not the one you think you should live. That might mean:

- ❖ Keeping a dining table big enough for every family dinner, even if it's not "minimal."

- ❖ Holding onto a single heirloom chair while letting go of the matching set.

- ❖ Choosing durable surfaces that reset easily after kids' homework or late-night projects.

You're not designing to impress—you're designing to support. Each piece should earn its place by function, comfort, or meaning. The rest is noise.

Heritage & Nature
My Foundation for Design

I learned early on that design wasn't just something you saw—it was something you felt. Afternoons spent in the barn at my friend Nicole's family ranch taught me that lesson. The smell of leather, the curved steel of bits, the layered wool rug beneath a saddle—every item was both functional and beautiful. Nothing was there by accident, and everything carried its weight with purpose.

That awareness was instilled more deeply in my own family. Both of my grandfathers, men of the U.S. Navy, brought craftsmanship into daily life. One built bridges in Hawaii, connecting landscapes and people. The other, a Navy Seabee mechanic, could construct buildings and bridges from the ground up. Their hands shaped more than wood and steel—they built a legacy.

Later, on the coast of Corpus Christi, I learned another side of design. We camped along North Padre Island, tracing paths through the dunes with seashells and driftwood, pausing to marvel at barnacles clinging fiercely to weathered wood. Even then, I noticed the details: textures, patterns, and resilience paired with fragility.

My heritage gave me builders; nature gave me textures. Together, they taught me that design becomes legacy—something that holds, supports, and inspires long after the moment it's built.

That inheritance is what I carry into Hivehouse Co. Designing with purpose means honoring the old while shaping the new, building bridges between heritage and modern living, permanence and change, function and beauty.

The lessons of heritage and nature became the blueprint for my design philosophy—simple, grounded, and intentional. Every step in *The Simplified Living Method* that follows is rooted in that foundation.

Whether it's simplifying, organizing, or styling, the goal is the same: to build spaces that function with purpose, flow with rhythm, and feel deeply aligned with the people who live within them.

A home designed with purpose tells a story: one of your rhythms, your values, and the life you're actively choosing.

Step 1. Simplify
Define the Mission

Before you buy another lamp or rearrange a sofa, pause. Write a one-sentence mission for the room:

> "This room is for unhurried dinners and conversation."

> "This space is for focused work and calm breaks."

That sentence becomes the anchor. Remove everything that doesn't serve it. Keep only what supports the mission: seating that fits bodies and lives, lighting that enhances the activity, surfaces that reset easily.

Key Principle: Start with the Why

When you know why a room exists, every choice—furniture, lighting, storage—becomes simpler.

Step 2. Organize
Map the Flow

Once the purpose is defined, map how the room moves. Look at paths of movement, spots where clutter collects, and the places where you stop and need something close at hand.

- ❖ Design zones to match routines: a reading chair with a lamp, a shelf near the ottoman for games, or a tray beside the couch for remotes.

- ❖ Place items where they're used: use drawer dividers, baskets, or hidden labels to keep the system invisible but intuitive.

- ❖ Reduce friction: hooks at the entry, a landing spot for mail, or bins near your desk.

Key Principle: Flow Shapes Feeling

Good design isn't about filling space; it's about guiding movement. When flow matches your rhythm, the room feels effortless.

Step 3. Style
Tell the Right Story

Styling is the layer where the story comes through. This is where you honor both utility and emotion: colors that soothe or energize, textures that welcome touch, objects that remind you of heritage or joy.

- ❖ Choose a palette that calms or sparks energy, depending on the mission.
- ❖ Layer textures: linens, woods, and wool—for warmth and depth.
- ❖ Leave negative space: it's not emptiness—it's breath.
- ❖ Curate meaning: display the pieces that carry a story; store the rest with care.

Mini Method: The 3-Anchor Rule

Give each room three anchors:

- ❖ A focal point (fireplace, artwork)
- ❖ A comfort element (textiles, lighting)
- ❖ A function support (storage, landing zone)

Everything else is optional.

A Note on Alignment

For years, I thought design was about appearance—matching colors, choosing the right furniture set, following what was "in." But every time I stepped into a room that actually worked, I realized it wasn't because it looked perfect. It was because it aligned.

Now, I design differently. I ask: *Does this serve the life we actually live here? Does it feel like us?* I think back to barns, bridges, and coastlines, to legacies built in steel and stories told through seashells. That's what designing with purpose is to me—spaces that serve, stories that last, homes that breathe.

Design Tip

If a piece constantly creates clutter, its design is wrong for the job—not you. Replace the system, not your standards.

Nature Note

The wind constantly reshapes dunes, yet their grasses hold them steady. Purposeful design works the same way—spaces can shift and adapt, but a few well-chosen anchors keep them rooted.

Inspired by Nature

Inspired by Nature

Where Beauty & Balance Already Exist

Inspired design is where beauty and balance already exist. It's not about chasing symmetry or staging a picture-perfect room—it's about noticing what feels grounded and alive. When a space honors the same principles nature does—strength balanced with delicacy, permanence balanced with change—it becomes more than functional; it becomes restorative.

Long before Hivehouse Co. existed, it was the bees that first taught me how nature designs with purpose. Their rhythm—equal parts work and rest—opened my eyes to balance as a living thing, not just a design principle. Observing their hive helped me see the broader natural world with the same respect: every part contributing, every detail functional, nothing wasted.

Design isn't just visual—it's sensory. It's the way sunlight warms a corner, how wood carries its grain like a fingerprint, how a simple stone on a shelf reminds you of a walk on the shore. A home inspired by nature tells a story: one of rhythm, renewal, and the quiet ways life always finds balance.

The Emotional Side of Nature's Design

Too often, we separate nature from our homes—treating it as something "out there" to be admired, not mirrored. But at its best, nature shapes how we feel indoors, too. A dark, cramped room can feel as stifling as an overcast day. A cluttered shelf can overwhelm the way a storm-clogged shoreline does. But when we honor balance—light with shade, texture with openness—spaces shift. You breathe easier. You move differently. You feel at home.

Permission to Design with Intention

Simplified Living gives you permission to design with nature's principles as your guide. That might look like:

- ❖ Keeping one sculptural branch in a simple vase, instead of a dozen knick-knacks.
- ❖ Choosing natural textures: linen, wood, clay—that age gracefully with use.
- ❖ Leaving negative space in a room, the way a meadow leaves room between trees and grasses.

You're not decorating to impress—you're creating balance that supports your rhythms. Each piece you keep should feel like sunlight through a window or air moving through an open door—welcomed, not forced.

Lessons Written in Nature

I learned early on that nature itself was a teacher of design. In 1983, when Hurricane Alicia roared through the Texas coast, I was only six. The storm was frightening—wind that howled, water that rose too quickly—but what stayed with me was what came after. Branches scattered across the street, fences broken down, driftwood carried inland. Some saw wreckage. I saw texture, story, and possibility.

Weeks later, I rode my bike to the trestles with friends, collecting what the storm had left behind—wood worn smooth by waves, twisted rebar jutting from the silt, even crawdads shifting through flooded ditches with shells streaked in rusts and blues. None of it felt accidental. A broken board, a shard of glass, a living creature—each carried story and texture, fragments of design waiting to be noticed.

I still remember how the sand clung to my skin, sticky and irritating, until one glimpse of sea glass made me forget the discomfort. Suddenly, the grit became part of the discovery, and I'd lose myself for hours, digging, sifting, and arranging what the tide had scattered.

That awareness only grew in the years that followed. On the North Padre Island coast, I lined seashells into winding paths, gathered driftwood spotted with barnacles, and studied the small things most people overlooked.

What stayed with me wasn't perfection, but the way beauty and grit existed together—resilience beside fragility, change pressed up against permanence. Those lessons shaped how I came to see design: not as flawless, but as something that endures, adapts, and reveals its meaning in layers.

That perspective is the foundation of *Simplified Living*. A home inspired by nature doesn't chase trends or symmetry—it honors what lasts while welcoming change. It's building bridges between organic and modern, strength and delicacy, resilience and renewal.

When we design with that awareness, our spaces stop trying to impress and start working in harmony with how we live. That is what makes them not just functional, but deeply restorative.

Nature's Design Principles

Those early encounters with storms, seashells, driftwood, and crawdads were more than childhood adventures. They were lessons in design that still guide me today:

Simplicity—Nature wastes nothing. Even in a storm's aftermath, every fragment has purpose. Our homes should echo that same clarity—holding only what is useful, meaningful, or truly beautiful.

Texture—From the mottled blues of a crawdad shell to driftwood softened by the tide, nature shows us that texture adds depth without demanding more. A home layered with natural texture feels grounded, not cluttered.

Adaptability—Dunes shift, ditches fill and empty, yet roots and grasses hold steady. Likewise, a home should flex with life's seasons while remaining anchored in what matters most.

Resilience—A fallen branch sprouts new shoots. Driftwood becomes sculpture. A scar in wood tells a story. Design isn't about resisting change but letting change deepen beauty.

Materials That Shape Us

The materials we choose carry both history and possibility. Each surface, each finish, carries its own story. Some remind us of what endures, while others point us toward what's possible. Choosing materials with intention means asking not just, *Does this look good?*, but also, *Does this support the way I want to live?*

Grounding Elements—Stone, wood, and clay hold the honesty of the earth—permanence, craft, and rhythm. They age with grace and remind us of what endures.

Modern Reflections—Brass, glass, and steel bring warmth, clarity, and strength. Brass softens light. Glass dissolves boundaries. Steel adds structure and resolve.

The Balance—Organic textures anchor us; modern surfaces sharpen us. Together, they create spaces that feel both rooted in history and alive with possibility.

Noticing Nature

Principles become powerful when they move from theory into practice. These simple exercises invite you to slow down, observe more carefully, and apply nature's design lessons in tangible ways.

Each one is less about adding and more about noticing—seeing what's already there, and letting those details guide how you shape your home.

Nature Walk Collection—Bring home one natural element—a branch, stone, or shell—and style it with purpose.

Light Audit—Notice how sunlight moves across your space throughout the day; reposition furniture or accents to complement it.

Material Mix—Combine grounding (wood, clay) and modern (brass, glass, steel) in one vignette. Observe how they balance.

Neighborhood Noticing—Photograph one architectural detail that catches your eye. Echo it at home through shape, color, or pattern.

A Personal Note on Resilience

I've always believed that the details we live with are never just details—they shape how we feel every day. When I hold a piece of driftwood in my hand or run my fingers across a clay bowl, I'm reminded that beauty and function can live in the same breath. These materials carry honesty. They soften with time, they show their wear, and they tell stories of time passing. They remind us that change is part of life, not something to resist, and that beauty and function aren't separate but rather intertwined.

In my own home, it's often the simplest details that bring the most grounding. A patch of morning sunlight across the table makes me pause. A clay mug that warms my hands. A stone I brought back from a walk. These aren't decorations for show; they're touchpoints that remind me to slow down, breathe, and notice.

Design Tip

Design doesn't begin with a full room overhaul—it starts with a single corner. Style one surface or reset one shelf. Those small anchors ripple outward and shift how the whole room feels.

Nature Note

A scar on a tree trunk, moss across stone, or new shoots sprouting from a fallen branch—nature never wastes change. Every shift adds to its story. What feels imperfect in your home may actually be a marker of life well-lived.

What I've carried from those early years—storms, shorelines, and small discoveries—is the understanding that beauty rarely arrives in perfect form. It's found in what endures, in what's weathered, and in the quiet reminders of resilience. Sifting through storm-tossed fragments, tracing seashell paths, and noticing the smallest details taught me to see possibilities where others might only see loss. That perspective still shapes how I see home today—not as something flawless, but as a place where simple choices and honest details quietly create the rhythm of a life well-lived.

Much like the hive itself, it's the small, steady rhythms—the tending, the restoring, the daily return to purpose—that create something lasting. That truth became the foundation of how I design, how I live, and ultimately, how Hivehouse Co. came to be.

Those early storms taught me to see the world differently—to look for rhythm and purpose in the aftermath of chaos. Years later, another storm—the Great Texas Freeze—would bring that lesson full circle. As snow fell and pipes burst, I found myself once again surrounded by family, by warmth, by conversation that sparked something new. In the hush of that cold, chaotic week, Lexi and I found ourselves doing what I'd always done as a child after a storm—sifting through the pieces, searching for beauty in what remained.

That morning, our laughter and ideas became their own kind of rebuilding. The notes we scribbled weren't just about homes—they were about hope. It struck me that the same principles that guided me on the coast all those years ago—resilience, rhythm, and renewal—were alive again, this time in the heart of a storm that would become the birthplace of Hivehouse Co.

Because beauty doesn't only emerge after the storm—it often begins there.

> Each surface, each finish, carries its own story.

Simplified Living Beyond the Home

Simplified Living Beyond the Home

Carrying Intention into Life

Simplified Living begins in our homes, but it doesn't end there. Once you've felt the calm of a room that truly works—where clutter no longer nags and design supports instead of distracts—you begin to crave that same clarity everywhere. Simplicity spreads. It reshapes how you approach your time, your commitments, even your relationships.

I grew up in a house that modeled two very different approaches to life. My dad's side of the family was militant in their cleaning and perfectionism, valuing order above all else. If you weren't ten minutes early, you were late. If chores weren't done, play was out of the question. One Saturday, desperate to get to my best friend Alicia's, I stashed clean clothes in the dirty hamper just to finish faster. My dad wasn't fooled. Before I even made it down the street, he'd already called her mom on the rotary phone to send me back. I was devastated—and I missed a Whitney Houston concert because of it.

My mom's side, though, was the opposite. They believed fun came first. I can still picture fifteen cousins crammed under forts made of brooms and king-sized sheets in the "front room," watching movies on the big square TV while popcorn littered the floor.

The adults stayed up late playing cards and Spoons, laughter spilling through the house while dishes piled in the sink. A clean kitchen could wait; joy couldn't.

Those extremes shaped me: order at all costs on one side, connection at all costs on the other. I learned that neither fully worked on its own. Too much order, and you miss the moment. Too much chaos, and you lose your grounding. Simplified Living is the balance—not perfection, not neglect, but intention.

Each time I choose what matters most, I find peace—and the steady reminder that enough is truly enough.

The Emotional Side of Everyday Life

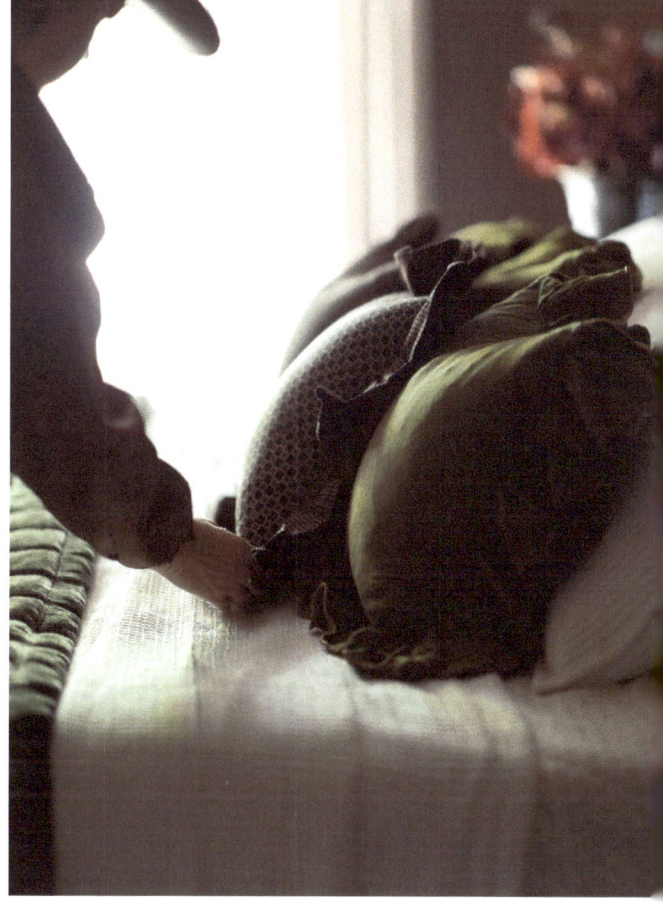

Clutter doesn't just live in closets—it also fills our calendars. Too much busyness can leave us disconnected from both others and ourselves. Every extra "yes" can stretch us thin, piling on stress until resentment and exhaustion follow. When we crowd our calendars, even the time we do have feels tainted, because we carry that weight with us. In that state, it's nearly impossible to sit peacefully with ourselves, make meaningful connections and memories with the people who matter to us most, or to feel free enough to fully enjoy life.

Sometimes the hardest part isn't what you take off your plate—it's the guilt you feel for doing so. Saying no can feel selfish. Slowing down can feel indulgent. Yet these feelings are part of the process, just like letting go of belongings we've outgrown. Balance doesn't happen by accident—it's chosen, one intentional decision at a time.

Permission to Live with Intention

One of the most powerful lessons *Simplified Living* offers is the permission to live simply. Permission to keep what matters in your home, and just as importantly, to keep what matters in your life.

That means:

- ❖ Permission to protect family dinners without apology.
- ❖ Permission to decline commitments that drain you, even if they look "good on paper."
- ❖ Permission to create margin in your days for rest, reflection, or simple joy.
- ❖ Permission to live for the life you're building now, not the one you think you should be chasing.

When you give yourself that permission, everything shifts. Life stops being a scramble to keep up and starts becoming a path you've intentionally chosen. The weight of "should" falls away, leaving room for what feels honest, grounding, and truly yours.

Principles That Travel Beyond Your Home

The principles that simplify a room also simplify a life. When we strip away what distracts, set systems that support, and choose rituals that restore, our days begin to feel lighter, more aligned, and more meaningful. Use the same trio—Simplify, Organize, Style—to create balance beyond your home.

Simplify—Define What's Draining You

Think of commitments like a cluttered drawer. If it's jammed with obligations, there's no room for what matters. Clear the excess: say no when needed, unsubscribe from what no longer inspires, unfollow the noise. Retire routines that no longer fit this season of life.

Organize—Create Flow in Your Days

Just like zones in a home, life benefits from rhythm. Batch errands instead of running daily. Hold weekly resets to set priorities and seasonal reviews to recalibrate goals. Protect your windows of deep focus. Build in margins so life feels breathable, not rushed.

Style—Design Your Days with Meaning

Styling your life is about layering what grounds you and inspires you. Add rituals that anchor you—an early walk, an evening cup of tea, or time each week for connection. Mark spaces for both rest and creativity. Choose habits and rhythms that reflect your values instead of reacting to pressure.

A Personal Note on Balance

What I learned from both sides of my family is that extremes never last. Perfection leaves no room to breathe, while chaos leaves no ground to stand on. Real life lives in the middle—the place where order steadies you and joy reminds you why it matters. The beauty exists not in clinging to one side or the other, but in noticing when the balance tips and being willing to recalibrate.

For me, balance shows up in everyday decisions. It's choosing when to push ahead and when to rest, when to welcome something new and when to protect what's already working. Some seasons call for structure; others call for openness. Balance doesn't ask for flawlessness—it asks for awareness. It's the ability to sense when something has become too heavy and to make a different choice. That slight shift has changed everything: instead of forcing myself to hold one way of being, I look for the path that brings both calm and momentum.

Design Tip

Just as a room needs walls, your days need edges. Define clear stopping points for work, and you'll create space for rest, play, and connection.

Nature Note

Waves never stay fixed—they advance and retreat. Balance works the same way. Some days call for forward motion; others require stepping back. Both movements are part of the design.

I've also come to see that balance isn't something you arrive at and keep forever. Just as seasons turn, so do our needs. What grounded me years ago doesn't always serve me now. Balance is the permission to revise—to release habits that weigh me down, to carry forward traditions that still matter, and to leave space for both practicality and meaning. A quilt stitched by my grandmother can root me as deeply as the planner that organizes my week. Both hold value, just in different ways.

What I understand now is that balance is not a finish line—it's a dialogue with life itself. It shifts as we shift, asking for both grace and attention. Some days it looks like clearing a single countertop; other days it looks like loosening the grip on an old expectation. Either way, balance is about deciding what's worth carrying and what can be set aside. Each time I choose what matters most, I find peace—and the steady reminder that enough is truly enough.

Conclusion

Conclusion
A Call to Live with Intention

Bees have always been my reminder that thriving communities are built on rhythm, clarity, and care. My grandfathers taught me that design is legacy, not trend—something you build to last. The coastlines of my childhood showed me that resilience and beauty can exist side by side. And from my parents' families, I learned that life needs both steadiness and spontaneity. Every lesson, every story, every thread of my history has led me here: to *Simplified Living*, a practice grounded in balance.

Simplified Living is not about scarcity. It's not about creating a picture-perfect space or cutting life down to bare bones. It's about aligning your surroundings, your time, and your energy with the life you want to live. A simplified life is not empty—it's full, but full of the right things. It is intentionally choosing what truly supports you—whether that's a room that feels calm at the end of the day, a tradition that still matters, or a relationship that brings you back to yourself.

Your home is more than four walls. It's the backdrop for conversations, milestones, laughter, grief, and every small moment in between. When it reflects what you value, it stops being just a container for your things and becomes a foundation for the way you live. A home designed with intention doesn't just serve your routines—it restores your rhythm and shapes the way you show up for the people and the world around you.

But *Simplified Living* doesn't stop at the threshold of a house. It extends to how you protect your time, the connections you choose to nurture, and the way you carry yourself through both work and rest.

It becomes a daily rhythm—a filter for decisions, both large and small—asking not, *What should I keep?* or *How should this look?* But *does this align with who I am and the life I want to live?*

**Enough clarity to notice what matters.
Enough structure to move with ease.
Enough beauty to remind you life
is meant to be lived.**

Simplified Living is not a final destination. It's an ongoing practice—a way of being that continues to evolve as seasons shift and life unfolds. I hope that the ideas and practices in these pages don't just inspire a reset in your home, but offer you a way of seeing: one that helps you choose more freely, live more lightly, and feel more at home in your life.

Author's Note

Thank you for walking this path with me. Writing this book has been less about creating a manual and more about tracing the lines of my own story—barns that smelled of leather and wool, coastlines scattered with shells and driftwood, chore charts that left no wiggle room, and cousin-filled forts where joy always came first. Each piece of that history shaped the way I see home, design, and life. Together, they became the foundation of Hivehouse Co. and the philosophy I now call *Simplified Living*.

I hope that these pages have given you more than ideas to try—that they've helped you notice your own spaces, your own habits, and your own story with a fresh perspective. *Simplified Living* was never about reaching some ideal version of life. It's about creating room for what matters most: the people you love, the moments that steady you, and the quiet reminders that enough really *is* enough.

If you're ready to take your next step, you don't have to do it alone. Hivehouse Co. exists to support the process through design services that reimagine your spaces, lifestyle tools like our hand-poured candles and reset kits, and the the Simplified Living™ Community by Hivehouse Co. on Facebook, where you'll find encouragement, accountability, and others walking the same path.

This is my invitation: start small, and start where you are. Reset one drawer, shift one routine, reclaim one corner of your home. Give yourself permission to release what weighs you down and keep what sustains you. Small choices made consistently create the kind of change that lasts.

Now it's your turn to carry these choices forward—beyond your walls and into your days. Let clarity shape your routines, let beauty remind you to pause, and allow connection to anchor you when life pulls in too many directions. Every choice you make—what you've kept, what you've released, and what you've chosen with care—is more than a step toward a lighter home. It's a step toward a fuller life, one grounded not in perfection, but in presence.

This book closes here, but your story with *Simplified Living* is just beginning. Keep choosing with intention, and let the balance you've built ripple outward into your time, your relationships, and your sense of self. Because in the end, *Simplified Living* isn't about less. *It's about enough—and enough is truly enough.*

With gratitude,

Tiffany Wheeler

Founder of Hivehouse Co.